WHEN I GR̲̲̲̲̲̲̲ ̲̲̲̲̲̲ ̲̲̲
I WANT TO BE...

Autobiography of
Richard Norman

Second Edition

Dedicated to
my children, my grandchildren,
and my great-grandchildren.

FORWARD

My father asked me from time to time in my life, when I would change careers, "What do you want to be when you grow up?"

I would change careers in the blink of an eye with no experience or education in the field.

Yet I would make it. Well. You'll see.

Chapter 1

When I grow up, I want to be...
an Opera Singer,
or an Artist, or a Commercial Artist...

Hi. I'm Richard Norman, or Dick Norman. I'm not really sure who I am. You see, my father always called me Richard, and my mother always called me Dick. I have always answered to either name. Mother often called me Dicky-boy which I grew to hate.

I was also a breech baby.
It wasn't my fault.
Don't blame me.
What a way to start a life.

Actually, I was born Richard Lee Norman, on September 15, 1929, in San Benito, Texas. The very next month, October, the Stock Market crashed. Don't blame me. It wasn't my fault. I had nothing to do with it.

My dad worked in a bank in Brownsville when I was born. I think he may have had a degree in banking from Texas University in Austin, Texas, but I am not sure. I know he attended Texas University at some time, and banking was his chosen profession all his life. Brownsville and San

Benito butted together as so many towns do in the Rio Grande Valley.

My dad was the smartest and wisest man I've ever known. He finished high school at such an early age that Texas University would not admit him, so he went back through high school a second and third time before he was deemed old enough to enter Texas University. I have all three of his diplomas from three different high schools.

After the stock market crash in March 1933, that Democrat, FDR, closed all the banks for a while, so my dad lost his job. I don't know how long he was out of work, but I remember dad telling me that the Democrats started a lot of Government work programs to put unemployed people back to work, but actually did nothing to improve the economy. Dad said he got a job digging ditches for $.50 a day. Dad never had anything good to say about FDR or Truman, or any other Democrats during his whole life. Dad was a Republican all his life. When I got old enough to vote I became a Republican and remain so.

When I was about a year old, mother entered me in a baby contest in Brownsville, Texas. I won first prize. The photo shows me and my parents. You can see my dad was a very small man, about 5'6", weighing about 100 pounds fully dressed in a business suit.

Our house was really my maternal grandparents' home in San Benito. My parents and I, and my new baby brother, Bert, were living with grandpa and grandma Waters. When I was about 3, I had my tonsils and adenoids removed. I do remember being in the hospital but have no unpleasant memories at all. I ate a lot of ice cream, and I have memories of a very special nurse. She was foreign, perhaps from Columbia, I'm not sure, maybe India. I thought she was so very pretty and kind and sweet. Her complexion was a golden tan. She brought me a box of chocolates from her country. I thought they were the best. She was my favorite nurse.

This is as good a place as any to tell about the maternal side of my family. I did not know them very well, since I spent most of my life with my father's side of the family. I have heard a few stories about them, and I had a few encounters with them over the years.

For example; grandpa Waters told about a time when he was Chief of Police in Brownsville and he came outside the police station where his office was located. He said he was walking along the city sidewalk when he noticed a young Mexican boy lying on the grass by the sidewalk. He was moaning and writhing around like he was hurting. Grandpa went to him, bent over him, touched him and asked him what was wrong. Suddenly, the young Mexican man jumped up and began fighting my grandpa. Like I said, grandpa waters were way over six feet, and more than 250 lbs., so he just pushed

This is me with my mom and dad.

the young man away. When he did, the young man ran away. Grandpa chased him for several blocks, and then felt a pain in his back. He felt his back, and there was blood on his hand. It turned out grandpa had nine knife wounds in his back. He never found the young man.

Grandpa Waters had six children; three boys and three girls. The oldest daughter was my aunt Bill (her name was Willie Dee, but I called her Aunt Bill), then there was my mother, Louise (Lavina Louise), and finally, aunt Lena (Lena Rae). The sons were Carroll, Jack (John Lamar), and Clarence. My aunt Bill lived to be 107, and aunt Lena is over 100 at this writing in 2018. Mother died at 94. I hardly remember my maternal grandmother at all.

The story is told that one night after midnight, uncle Carol heard a noise outside the house. He got up and looked out the living room window to see two Mexican boys trying to steal grandpa Waters' car – his "Chief of Police" car. Carroll woke grandpa and the other two boys up (all the boys were in their 20s). One of the Mexican boys was in the driver's seat with his head down, trying to get the ignition to start when grandpa walked up to his car window and asked, "What are you boys trying to do?" The Mexican boy raised up with a gun in his hand and stuck the business end in grandpa's face. But before he could fire, grandpa grabbed the end of the pistol and turned it up. The bullet went through the middle of grandpa's right hand. The Mexican boys and grandpa had a shootout over that car, and my three uncles ran away (they didn't have any guns). Uncle Jack said he was so scared he ran to a big tall fence and he could not remember going over it, or around it, or through it, but he went to look at it the next day, and two boards were missing. They never bothered to tell the outcome of the gunfight, but grandpa Waters had a scar on both sides of the middle of his right hand.

Uncle Jack was my favorite uncle. He was "tall, dark and handsome." He had black curly hair, a reddish complexion, and a muscle-bound build like Charles Atlas (known in that time as the best in the world). He was over 6'. His arms were really huge. His long-sleeved shirts were special made to fit his big biceps. A normal shirt, he could split. He was a faithful member of the Lord's church, and, eventually, became an elder. Grandpa Waters' girls were all faithful members of the church all their lives. Uncles Carrol and uncle Clarence were never faithful Christians.

Uncle Carroll was about as strong as uncle Jack. One day, the two of them were traveling somewhere, and they had a flat. The car they were driving was an old Model A. It had a spare tire, but no jack. Uncle Carroll picked up the part of the car with the flat tire, while uncle Jack changed the tires. Just as they were about done, uncle Carroll let the car slip out of his hands, and it fell on uncle Jack's left hand, catching his first two fingers at the top two joints, crushing them. Uncle Jack pulled his hand away, tore away the remaining straggling flesh, and held the nubs of his two fingers tightly until they could get to a doctor.

The hurricane:

When I was about 3 or 4 years old, I remember my mother was extremely nervous. She would walk through the house, and go into the living room, sit on the couch, and look out the window. I remember running to the couch, climbing up on it, standing by mother, and looking out the window with her. I asked her what she was looking at, and she said, "Nothing." But I heard the adults talking, and I recall the gist of the conversation.

They were talking about the gathering clouds in the sky, and spoke of the way the trees would shake, and grow still, shake and grow still. I watched out the window and saw what they were talking about. I noticed a row of small, young trees as they would shake and grow still, shake and grow still. The adults said the things they were noting indicated the coming of a hurricane. Back in the early 1930s, weather reports were virtually non-existent, but somehow the adults knew a big hurricane was about to hit the Rio Grande Valley where we were living. That wasn't my fault either.

The hurricane finally came. It was a very scary storm to me, but mother assured me we would be alright. But when the hurricane was tearing my grandparent's wooden house apart, and the kitchen portion blew away, we were forced to leave. Arrangements were made to go to a friend's brick house on a hill. It was thought to be able to survive the hurricane.

Grandpa Luther Waters was a huge man, I think about 6' 6". I remember him getting a big 4X4 to prop a car door open against the fierce hurricane winds, so we could get into the car to get to higher ground to escape the flooding of the hurricane waters.

The car was fairly high off the ground in those days. All cars had "running-boards" on both sides of the car to aid us in climbing up into the seats. Along the way, I remember looking out the car window and seeing a small garage. Suddenly one wall lifted up, then the roof flew up, followed by the other wall, and they all blew away in the wind. Inside the small garage was an old truck. It began rolling over and over. It seemed to me the little garage was barely large enough to fit the little pickup truck.

Our car crept through waters up above our running-boards and almost into our car until we reached a brick home of friends who invited us to weather the storm with them on a little hill.

All houses then had wallpaper on their walls and even on ceilings. I remember the ceiling paper having bulges where the paper had drooped down all over the ceiling because of water leaking through the roof. The adults climbed up 6' ladders to punch holes in the ceiling paper to let the water drip into pans that dotted the floors everywhere. The only place in the house that was dry was a square hallway in the middle of the house. There were no bulges in the ceiling paper there. Mother rolled small carpets to block every entrance to the hallway to keep the water from going into the hallway. It was there on that dry floor that mother put my baby brother Bert. He old enough to sit up on that floor I remember after the hurricane that one of my uncles waded in water up to his waist to go buy cigarettes at some store.

Moving to Austin, Texas.

I remember mother and dad packing all our worldly possessions into a two-seater, Willis Whippet automobile, and all four of us crowded into the front seat (the back seat was a rumble seat that folded up from where a trunk would have been. A few of our possessions were crammed into that seat area). Dad drove us from San Benito to Austin; the State Capital. I think I was 4 years old when we moved in with my grandparents in Austin. "Nanny," my grandmother's mother also lived there.

Grandpa and grandma Norman had a large house. We lived with them until I was 17. I remember that my baby brother, Bert, could barely sit up alone when we were in the hurricane, so he must have been less than a year old.

I don't remember the trip to Austin, but I do remember that the highway was only one lane in either direction. It must have taken several days travel to go from Brownsville to Austin.

Most of my life, especially my growing-up years, I believed my grandpa Norman was a Gospel Preacher. I never heard him say anything different till the day he died. Anytime he was asked, "Mr. Norman, what do you do?" He would always reply, "I'm a Gospel Preacher." I was grown and married before I learned that he often made the major part of his income in other ways.

Eventually, I learned that for a number of years, Grandpa Norman operated the largest Kansas City Life Insurance office in Austin. I also learned that he had started the Northside church of Christ from nothing. He also had

12

started the Southside church of Christ in south Austin from nothing. Both churches grew substantially, and when we moved to Austin, Grandpa was the fulltime preacher at Northside. I never knew any different. I don't know what churches paid him. He never seemed to care how much he was paid. I do remember going to his Kansas City Life Insurance Office, and meeting his secretary, but I never put any of it together. I thought his only job was preaching at Northside.

One day grandpa told this story:

> One morning, grandpa's secretary at his insurance office was late to work. It was obvious she was very upset and had been crying. Grandpa was very concerned and sympathetic. He had her sit down and tell him what was troubling her. She said that she and her husband had gone to a carnival the night before, and that they had visited a fortune-teller. She said that the fortuneteller lady had told them that her husband was going to die within the next six months. Then she burst into tears. Grandpa quieted her down again and then asked her if the fortuneteller lady was still in town. She said that she was. Grandpa said, "Well, this evening, you and your husband go back to see that fortuneteller lady and ask her where your husband will die, and just don't ever go there."

Grandpa always seemed to have plenty of money. We always had plenty to eat, and grandpa always drove a big, fine car. Grandpa always had a housekeeper to clean house and help grandma, and he insisted she be a white woman. She worked every day.

Everybody said I looked like my grandpa when I was little. Mother often told of taking me to grandpa's insurance company office in downtown Austin. She said that when she would get on the elevator in the building with me in her arms, people would say, "Oh, I bet I know whose little boy

13

that is." Mother said she would answer, "I bet you don't, but I bet you know who his grandfather is."

My grandmother, who was an invalid and bedridden, had me come in from play every afternoon to come to her bedroom so that she could read the Bible to me. It was a time I enjoyed very much. I don't know what she did to make it such a treat, but I remember that it was a time I always looked forward to, never tired of those grand Old Testament stories. I learned a lot of the Bible from her in those early years.

In those early years, I didn't pay much attention to what was going on around me because I loved to draw so much. Mother was busy with my baby brother. (His name was John Albert, but my parents called him Bert.) Mother told me, after I was grown, that I was never a problem when I was a child. If my mother was busy, and if she needed to do something with me to keep me busy and out of the way and content for a good long time, she would find a good pencil with a good point and a few sheets of blank paper. Finally, she would set me down in the middle of the kitchen floor (it was smooth linoleum), and I would draw for hours.

I am deeply ashamed to admit that in those years, I hardly remember my brother. I truly lived in my own little world. I am so very sorry for my sinful neglect of Bert.

I remember that when grandpa would come home every afternoon, he would seek me out like I was somebody special, pick me up, and stand me on our big dining room table. He would ask me what all kinds of things I had done that day. I would tell him I had been hauling dirt all day, and I was very tired. We would talk about that a few minutes, and then he would ask me to sing him a song. I would sing at the top of my voice, and he would just rave about what a great singer I was (at 4 or 5 or 6 years old). He would do that most every day, and I loved it – I loved to sing.

At church at times, I remember grandpa getting me up in front of the whole church to stand by him and help him lead singing. I was so small I could hardly hold a songbook in my arms, but I sang my heart out. I did that on a regular basis. I don't know if I could carry a tune when I was 4, 5, or 6, but he also took me with him often when he drove places. I don't know where we would go, but he would sing and get me to sing with him. Grandpa never said I couldn't carry a tune. So far as I knew, I could always carry a tune. But at some point, early in my life I know I could carry a tune because he started teaching me to sing and to read music - shaped notes. (solfege):

Grandpa taught Singing Schools for churches, and I attended many of them. By the time I was a teenager, I was an excellent song leader, and often lead singing for large churches. Since I had been in front of the whole church since I was 4 or so, I have never experienced stage-fright.

Across the street from Grandpa's house was a nicer looking, two-story house where my first best friend lived. His name was Bub Merrell. We were the same age and were often called Night and Day. Bub had very black hair, and mine was as white a blond as my skin was white. People could hardly tell where my hair ended, and my skin began. I don't remember us ever in a fuss or fight. We played together just about every day, either at his house or mine, but nearly always outside in the backyard. We both liked to draw "little boy's play houses." They were very elaborate, with all kinds of tunnels and tree houses and hide-outs and stuff that went on for pages and pages in our tablets. We would buy Big Chief tablets for a nickel - they had 100 pages. We would draw for hours.

We would eat at each other's house and have sleepovers. His dad was rich - he was an airline pilot. His mother served food I was not used to even seeing as a poor boy, much less eating. She served what I called "little green balls" (English peas). (We ate red beans (pinto beans) at my house.) Bub's mother would also put "little bushes" on my plate. I learned they were not for eating, but for making my plate of food look nice. I learned that Bub Jr.'s mother, who had snow-white hair, had had it since she was 20 years old. When I was a little older, I went with Bub and his mother to the airport for some reason, and big Bub, Sr. (his dad) wanted to take me and Bub Jr. for a ride in his personal plane. I said, "I could go up if I really wanted to, but I just didn't want to right now."

Actually, Bub, Jr. and his parents were living with big Bub's parent's house. Bub's grandpa hand built wooden speed-boats with internal engines. He built them in his garage. They were sleek and beautiful. I imagine he made a fortune - his house looked really expensive.

The Trolley car stop was at the end of the block we lived on, and we lived in the middle of the block. Later on, when busses came along, they came right down our street. There was a little "mom & pop" grocery store at the end of our block and around the corner. I remember buying a quart of milk for a nickel and a loaf of bread for a nickel. Mother said that if she sent me to the store for 3 things, I would forget at least one, if not 2 of the 3 things. We had a neighbor lady that passed our house on her way to the grocer. On her way back, she would be carrying cokes, and I would hear mother say, "Tsk, tsk." It was a long time before I heard that cokes

This is grandpa as I first remember him.

had originally contained cocaine, but I don't know if they did in the 1930s.

When we lived with my grandparents, it was one of the happiest times of my life. Grandpa was jovial all the time. He woke up boisterous, singing hymns and telling everyone good morning. We always had breakfast together as a family (seven of us), often lunch, and dinner in the evening.

Grandpa loved to tell jokes and funny stories - he could tell one after another all the time. We would all gather around his big radio each evening in his bedroom to listen to all the great programs like - **Bob Hope**, **Jack Benny**, **Fibber McGee & Molly**, etc.

Fibber McGee and Molly.

Grandma was a small bag of bones. One night when I was about 10, I had a nightmare, and cried out in the night. I woke up suddenly and saw a skeleton in a white gown with a pale face and wild hair - it was coming into my room. I started to scream, but then I saw it was grandma. She nearly scared the life out of me. My grandmother Norman died in her early 70s.

I remember several times friends of my parents would come visit us in Austin, and I recall our going down to Brownsville to see Royce Russell and his wife who seemed to be named Russell. That was the only name she was ever called by as far as I remember. They had an adopted daughter just a couple of years younger than I. I remember that when our two families were together, we always had a big treat; vanilla ice cream floats with ginger-ail.

My first school was just up the street about three blocks; Baker Elementary. There is a lot I do not remember about those days. I do remember a very big, tall, fat boy being bullied on the playground by a short, muscular kid that cursed at him, punched him, and made fun of him. I could not understand why the big guy didn't defend himself. I was worried about that event, but it soon dissipated. It is the only such incident I remember. I was never bullied in school. I was a scrawny little guy but seemed to be well liked.

I remember one of my favorite classes in school. We went in, sat down, and our teacher opened a record player, and played classical music for us. She would tell us what it was, who wrote it, and what the music was about, and the story of the composer's life. I dearly loved that class, and I loved that music, but grandpa always said, **"Classical music is music you can neither whistle nor hum and wouldn't if you could."**

It was grandpa, however, who introduced me to classical music and opera. He didn't like it. He always listened to **The Firestone Hour** which was a musical program of semi-classical music. Near the end of their program, they would feature some classical work. Often it was an aria by a great current opera singer. I was the only one in the family that loved to hear classical music and grand opera. I also loved the popular music of the 1930s and 1940s.

I have no idea how I learned about art, but somehow, I learned a lot about drawing, color, fine art and commercial art, and developed a lot my artistic skills on my own before I started first grade. I can't imagine my parents helping me, or anyone else helping me. I did not know anyone who knew anything at all about art. I was a poor student in school except for art, music and English.

I remember selling The Saturday Evening Post magazines door to door when I was about 8. Someone would bring me a stack of Post magazines, and I had a cloth sack carrier. I would go up and down the streets around my block and try to sell them to people. I made a few pennies, I guess, but I got to read the magazine. In that time, the great illustrators of the US were featured in the Post led by Norman Rockwell. That group of illustrators had a correspondence school to teach commercial art and illustration. I read a lot in the

Saturday Evening Post. I decided at the age of 8 that I wanted to be a commercial artist like Norman Rockwell and others in the Post when I grew up.

When I went into my very first art class in grade school, the teacher wanted to teach the class about the color wheel. She started by explaining about "Primary Colors," red, yellow and blue. While she talked to the class about how mixing red and yellow together would make the color orange, etc., I had a box of crayons, so I drew a color wheel, and put **all** the colors in my crayon box in their proper order for a complete color wheel. Somehow, I already knew what colors mixed together would make what colors. I don't remember how I already knew that.

My teacher saw what I had done and was amazed that I knew so much more about art than she was going to teach to the class, so she allowed me to work independently while she taught the rest of the class.

That was pretty much the way it went for me in art classes the rest of my way through school. It seemed I somehow already knew how to draw and paint and needed no instruction from a teacher. My works won art contests all through school from the very beginning. There didn't seem to be anything in art I couldn't do. In high school, I would sit in library class and draw portraits of pretty girls that sat across the table from me. I would use art pencils, and I would do careful shading, and the pictures would look exactly like the girls. The girls were very impressed.

MY FIRST ART CONTEST

When I was in the 3rd grade, I entered my first art contest. It was a city-wide contest, including all schools in Austin, Texas. I won first prize. The prize was a ticket to a children's play that came to Austin every year. That picture is somewhere in the debris of my stuff. I have seen it recently but have no idea where it is. It was no big deal for me to win first prize in art contests. I knew just exactly how good I was as an artist.

I don't remember when this next part happened, but our family (dad, mother, me and Bert) moved out of grandpa's house into a new, white house in South Austin. It was at the top of a hill, not far from the Colorado River. It had no grass or shrubs in the yard, just black dirt that turned to mud when it rained. The house was extremely small. The only heat in winter was from a pot-belly stove in the small living room. When it was very cold in the winter time, you could feel very warm on your side next to the stove if you were very close to it but the side of you that was not facing the stove was freezing cold. It was the most miserable place I ever lived.

Dad had a great big car, and the garage was behind the house. One night, dad stopped out front to let us all out of the car before he parked it in the garage. Mother was just in front of me and about to reach the front door. I think mother's younger sister was visiting us, and she was behind me. Suddenly, mother yelled, "Bert!" We all turned toward the street to look for him. He was a toddler at the time, and we all saw Bert at the front bumper of dad's car just as dad started to drive away. Mother and aunt Lena screamed! Mother and Lena had their arms full of stuff that they threw into the air. We saw Bert's little body go under the car, and the big car go completely over him. But the screams caused dad to stop. Mom and Lena ran to the car, and dad got out, and they scooped Bert up into mom's arms and ran into the house. I was too young to understand all the confusion that followed, and I don't remember what all happened, but none of the wheels rolled over Bert's body. All he had were a few bumps and bruises and scrapes and cuts.

Across the street from our little house lived a family I remember as a bunch of riffraff's. Their name was Firebacher, and one of their boys about my age shot me in the back with a bee-bee rifle. It went into my flesh, and we never got the pellet out. Many years later, I had a large cyst removed from my back, but no pellet was found.

Bert had a lot of problems with having abscesses in his ears. Eventually he lost his hearing as a result. This added to our living in two different worlds, and not being as close as brothers should be. Bert went to a school for the deaf in South Austin and lived there. He grew up there and lived in that silent world. We did not live in south Austin very long and moved back into grandpa's house in a district called Hyde Park.

I don't remember much about when I was a child. My father told me many times over the years that I seemed to live in a little dream-world all my own. I do remember playing in the dirt in a round structure made for growing flowers that was made of cement with small rocks. I had several tiny cars and trucks, and pretended I was hauling dirt to make roads and hills in the structure.

I remember getting in a fight one day with a neighbor boy down the street. It was the only fight I ever had. I was about six I think. I also remember two big boys next door playing catch with a baseball in the yard by their house. They each had baseball gloves. In the winter they threw a football to each other.

Their name was Smith, and their father was my barber. I remember grandpa taking me to him for a haircut, and he had just raised the price of his haircuts from a dime to 12 cents. Grandpa thought it was outrageous. In those days a man could get a shave and a haircut for two-bits (a quarter). I also recall my great grandmother saying that she thought kissing a man without a beard would be like kissing a woman which she deemed disgusting.

Born again...

24

The Bible and the church were absolutely first place in our

house, and religion, the church and the Bible were often discussed. Our church had gospel meetings in the spring and fall of every year, and they were always two to three weeks in duration.

We, as a family (mother, dad, and I) attended every time the doors of the church building were open for a service of any kind. Of course, grandpa attended. Grandma was seldom well enough to attend. Nanny, grandma's mother, seldom attended. She was in her 90s. We would also often attend gospel meetings at other congregations nearby. In the 1930s, and 1940s, preachers often, if not always, preached 45 minutes to an hour or more. Consequently, I heard **LOTS** of preaching as I was growing up. In those years, many preachers, especially in gospel meetings, used large charts and visual aids to illustrate their sermons.

At home, as I was growing up, I had countless discussions with my father and grandfather about the Bible, the church, Christianity, and a host of related subjects. We had Bible classes at church on Sunday mornings, Sunday evenings before the evening worship, and on Wednesday nights. I was never encouraged to be a daily Bible reader in those days, but to study for my Bible classes three times a week; I was a virtual daily Bible reader. I was, however, encouraged to memorize certain passages of Scripture. Sometimes whole chapters of the New Testament like the 13th chapter of 1st Corinthians (the "love" chapter of the New Testament).

What I had learned by the time I was 12 years old:

Church history:

I had learned a lot about general church history, and I was taught the history of Christianity, and how The Roman Catholic Church is not the original church that you read about in the New Testament, but a perversion of that church. There were big charts presented with documentation in church history, and in the New Testament. The charts were printed on bed sheets and on large sheets of oil cloth. I had questioned and talked about these things with preachers and with my father and grandfather. I was shown the history books in my grandfather's personal library. I have such history books in my personal library today, plus, I have many books from my grandpa's personal library.

I was taught about the Reformation era. On the many large charts brought by many evangelists through my growing up years, I learned who Reformers were, and that they merely wanted to reform the Catholic Church. I learned about the formation of other Denominations. I knew when in history they were begun, why and where. I knew they all taught the doctrines of men – they were false doctrines. We were told that none of the Denominations existed in New Testament times, or before the dates given for their beginning in history. All the documentations were listed on the charts, so anyone could check the truth of what was being preached. I have such history books today.

None of these were the true church that you read about in the New Testament, but were churches devised and invented by men. They each taught a different doctrine to each other, and we would learn that none of them taught the doctrine of the church in the New Testament. Then those preachers would preach about the church you read about in the New Testament. They would use big charts to help us understand that New Testament church. I had heard these things over and over and over again for years.

I was taught Restoration History:

I was taught about the New Testament church. In the New Testament book of Romans, chapter 16, verse 16, the apostle Paul speaks of *"The churches of Christ."* Obviously, in the first century, if there were many in the plural, there were some in the singular – a church of Christ. If not, why not?

The preachers that came to hold our gospel meetings preached about **Restoration History**, a movement, not to reform anything, but to restore the original church that Christ built. Its pattern is found in the New Testament. Jesus said in Matthew 16:18, "I will build My church." His church, the church of Christ began on the day of Pentecost that you can read about in the New Testament in the book of Acts, chapter 2. Big charts showed all the Bible passages that told of the church in its prophecy and in its fulfillment. The charts revealed how that church that Jesus built was to be organized with elders and deacons, how it should worship with singing, praying, giving, communing (with the Lord's Supper – the unleavened bread and the fruit of the vine), and preaching of the gospel, what it's mission was – to edify itself, to do benevolent works, and to evangelize the world. The New Testament told how we were to be saved – that we were to hear the good news of the gospel of Christ, how that He had died for our sins on the cross and was buried, and that He was raised from the dead on the third day by the glory of the Father, and that He ascended into heaven to sit at the right hand of the Father to reign as Christ our King. We must believe in Him with all our heart, repent of all our sins, be buried with Him in baptism for the remission of all our sins, and raised to walk in newness of life as a Christian, nothing more, and nothing less.

> *By the time I was 12, I had seen and heard these teachings, and heard them explained in infinite detail inside out and upside down, until I knew I needed to be baptized into Christ in order to "put on Christ," and as Jesus said, "**to be born again.**" I remember crying one night in my bed over my sins, and the next Sunday morning, when I was 12 years old, grandpa baptized me for the remission of my sins at the Northside church of Christ where he was the preacher.*

Soon after my baptism, my father became an elder of the congregation. He was only 35 years old, but he made a great elder and served as such for 40 years.

I still believe all these things because the Bible still teaches what it has always taught and has never changed. The Bible is right. It has always been right, and it will always be right until Jesus comes again. *We* may get things wrong and mess things up now and then, but we can always go back to the Bible, and find the original pattern, and put things right again.

The church of Christ is the only church in the world that makes any attempt at all to follow the pattern of the church that is revealed in the New Testament.

I remember attending every service of the church each week, and I remember many gospel meetings and hearing some of the most prominent preachers of that day. We had two two-week gospel meetings every year, and my family took me to many gospel meetings of other churches of Christ within driving distance. I heard a very great number of sermons in those years.

Every morning over the school intercom system we stood and recited The Pledge of Allegiance to our US flag. Then we were led in prayer over the intercom by a student. I did not approve of those prayers at all. They were virtually always led by kids of various denominations, even led by girls on occasions. I would say my own prayer in my mind because I f believed prayers led by one who belonged to a denomination were an abomination to God, especially I believed that no female should ever lead a public prayer anywhere.

Chapter 2

A remarkable story!

Grandpa told me that when he came to Texas, at the age of 19, there were only 25 church of Christ preachers in the entire state, and he knew them all. Texas is 1,000 miles across in two directions.

The year was 1900, and grandpa began to preach the gospel of Christ in Texas along with the other 25 preachers. There were no churches of Christ to support any of them, so they all had to find ways to support themselves, and preach for free, and establish churches of Christ in Texas. Grandpa supported himself by breaking horses. All they had was the old King James Version of the Bible. I have no idea how many churches Grandpa established from scratch, but I have visited many through the years. I was told he established 100 congregations or more in his lifetime.

Grandpa preached mostly in and around central Texas, but sometimes he would venture into West Texas. Baptizing, of course, always by total immersion in water. He said that sometimes the only available water for him to baptize respondents in in West Texas, were a rancher's water tanks for their cattle. Grandpa said that West Texas could get so hot and dry that the water tanks could be so shallow he nearly had to "stand on their necks" to get them under.

Before grandpa died in 1975 about a month prior to his 94th birthday. He had lived to see the entire state of Texas totally evangelized, and so covered with churches of Christ, so that virtually every little town in Texas had a congregation, and still has today. Of course, those few preachers did not do the job alone. Many other Christians (members of the churches of Christ) came to Texas to help them over the years, and those that were converted, converted others.

When grandpa was 84, he attended a World Mission Forum in Dallas, and learned of all the great mission efforts of churches of Christ that were being done all over the world at that time. He was so moved by what he heard, he told me, "Dick. You know, if I was a young man, that's exactly what I would be doing." I said, "Grandpa, what are you talking about? That's exactly what you did."

Back in those days, most people were converted by preaching, not by one-on-one Bible study. I can remember many people of all ages, young and old, responding to the invitation at gospel meetings to be baptized. There was a church of Christ preacher named Ben Franklin (yes, a descendent of the great patriot). Historians claim Franklin baptized over 10,000 in gospel meetings in his lifetime. That was not uncommon. Whole denominational congregations were sometimes converted, and became a church of Christ, changing their sign out front of their building.

Another church of Christ preacher with a rather famous name was Walter Scott, a descendent of the great English author, Sir Walter Scott. He too baptized about 10,000 or more in his preaching lifetime. It was Scott, I believe, who first conceived the idea of singing a song of invitation. Up until then, the invitation was offered by the preacher, and everyone just sat in silence as people responded.

Grandpa said that he was preaching in a small farming community one time, and in the middle of the night, he heard a knock on the front door. He got out of bed, went to the door, and found a young country boy with his girlfriend. They wanted grandpa to marry them right then. He invited them in, went to get dressed, got grandma up to be a witness, and they had all necessary legal papers, so he performed their wedding ceremony in the living room that very night.

Luther Norman, my grandpa, as a young man.

After the ceremony, the country boy sidled up to grandpa and said, "Brother Norman, how much do I owe you for this here now weddin'?" Grandpa, always facetious, said, "Why don't you just give me what you think she's worth?" The boy stood on one foot and then the other looking her over. Then he reached in his pocket and pulled out a fifty-cent piece and handed it to grandpa. Grandpa said he turned to look at the scraggly little girl and gave him a quarter change.

Grandpa told about holding a gospel meeting in a small country town, and after the Sunday morning service, he was invited home with a family for Sunday dinner. In the late afternoon, just before time for the Sunday evening service, the lady of the house asked grandpa if he wanted anything to eat before worship. Grandpa said, "No, thank you. It affects my preaching if I eat before I preach."

Later, after the evening service, grandpa asked the lady how she liked his sermon. She said, "You might as well a' et'."

Chapter 3

Climbing fool's hill...
My teenage years...

My dad always referred to the teenage years as "Climbing Fool's Hill."

As a result of my baptism, I was presented with a Bible. I still have that Bible, and it is the first Bible I ever read straight through from cover to cover.

Also, after my baptism, my dad was selected and appointed as an elder of the Northside church of Christ in Austin, Texas. Dad was only 35 years old at the time. That was very young for a man to serve as an elder of the church, but as I have said many times, I think my dad was not only one of the smartest men I have ever known, I think he was one of the wisest men I have ever known. I have seen him in action and under fire (so to speak) as an elder many times, and he was ever able to "maintain the unity of the spirit in the bond of peace." He knew the Bible like the back of his hand. I have known only one other elder as young as my dad, and he, too, was wise and knowledgeable beyond his years.

One Sunday evening, I told my dad I was not going to church. He said, "Why? What's the matter? Don't you love the Lord?" He reminded me of just how much Christ loved me, and what He had done for me. He went on to talk about the church being Christ's body, and the way we treated the church was the way we were treating Christ's body. He reminded me that God, the Father, Christ, and His Holy Spirit would be present for our worship, and didn't I want to be present to worship them? What was it, he wondered, was more important to me than being present with my brothers and sisters in Christ as we met for worship?

Then he said I should go to my room and talk to my Lord about it, and explain it all to Him, and then if I still felt it was all right to miss Sunday night services, then it would be fine with him (my dad).

That was just a part of his reasoning with me, but he fixed my "want to" once and for all, forever. I have never found anything in life more important than meeting my appointments with my Lord for worship. I fully understood the Scripture, "Seek ye *first* the kingdom of heaven."

The year I turned 12 years old, was also the year Pearl Harbor was attacked by the Japanese, and America entered the conflict of World War II. I heard FDR's declaration of war over my school's PA system during a class.

I don't know who started the rumor that FDR led America out of the Great Depression, but I was led to believe that it was World War II that did that job, not anything FDR did.

My dad worked as Federal Bank Examiner during the war years and did a lot of traveling. After the war, dad went to Rutgers University and got some kind of degree or something that he said was equivalent to a PhD in Economics. It helped him in his banking career.

I remember my dad was very cold natured. He seemed to be cold all the time, but we lived in Austin, Texas, a very hot climate most of the time. Still, I remember he used to say, "Body temperature is 98.6, and if it gets any cooler than that, it is too cold."

We continued living in grandpa's house until I was 17, but I will just mention various and sundry things during that time period, and a few things I have missed along the way. Grandpa was a great singer. He had an enormous tenor voice. He was better known in the brotherhood as a singer than a preacher (truth be told, he was not a very dynamic preacher). He could lead a very large crowd of people outdoors, without a sound system, and be easily heard. It was a beautiful, huge voice, and a very wide range.

In their younger years, both grandpa and grandma Norman had been school teachers. They had both taught English Grammar. Grandpa had become a Principal of a school, but I don't know more than just that. Both grandpa and grandma taught me English Grammar, mostly just in and through daily conversation, so well, that I always made good grades in English, but especially in Grammar. For example, if I were to say to grandpa, "I'm going to go lay down." Grandpa would say to me, "Chickens lay; people lie."

Many years later, when I was in my early 20s, I took English Grammar at SMU, and I truly believe I knew it well enough to have taught it. I made straight A's in college grammar.

I was a very poor student in school all the way through high school. I remember dad trying to help me with my math homework in the evenings when I was in grade school. It, of course, was so clear and easy for him, but for the life of him, he could not get it into my head. His frustration was palpable.

When I started first grade, I was not allowed to enter until I was almost 7 because my birthday was September 15. Then, in junior high, I failed to pass several semesters. When it was time for my high school class to graduate, I lacked a half credit, so I waited the whole summer until the fall semester and was graduated at mid-term. I was 19.

When I entered Junior High School, it was near Texas University, and I had to ride a bus to and from school. At the age of 12, I had reached my full height and never grew any more. I was one of the tallest boys and played center on

35

our basketball team. When I got to Senior High, even some girls were taller than I.

Austin High School was really Stephen F. Austin High School, and it was on the corner of 11th Street in downtown Austin. We lived on 43rd Street. I had to take a bus to school. I would get off the bus at 11th Street downtown and walked downhill many blocks to my school. I never thought anything about those problems. I was a very happy and content teenager.

I made all As in high school in art, chorus, drama, speech, English, creative writing, and journalism. I only had problems with math, science, history, geography, social studies, and stuff like that. I just didn't want to study those courses in high school.

My first voice lessons:

When I was 16, I began taking voice lessons from the best voice teacher in Austin, Texas. Her name was Mrs. Broman (I never knew her first name). She charged $10,00 per hour. In 1946, $10.00 an hour was an enormous amount of money, unheard of. I only took half-hour lessons, for my young untrained voice could not endure an hour of such rigorous training.

I've taken voice lessons throughout my life until age 78, but I have never had as great a teacher as Mrs. Broman. She taught me how to breath, get my voice out of my throat and project it into the roof of my mouth and near my front teeth.

It was a struggle to learn to breathe properly. She had me lie on a hard, flat surface and relax. Then she pointed out that my chest was not expanding when I breathed, but my back and sides around my waist expanded. That, she said, was breathing from my diaphragm. I was not to breath from my

36

chest, but from my diaphragm. Learning to do that standing up was a slow process to become natural for me, but since then, I always breathe from my diaphragm when I sing even as I write this account. I learned how to sing properly in those 5 years with Mrs. Broman. I know how to project my voice with great power, but almost no effort. I learned to LET my voice sing, not MAKE it sing. I can sing for hours and never get hoarse from singing.

I have always loved to sing. Singing has always been a very large part of my life.

You may not believe a high school would offer such courses as art, chorus, drama, speech, English, creative writing, and journalism. Well, English of course, but those other courses were marvelous, and the teachers were great. I really learned a lot in those courses from those teachers that have helped me all my life.

Growing up in grandpa's house, I had learned lots of Bible, lots of religious history, etc., and I had learned how to sight-read Solfege (once you learn that, it is easy to learn to read regular round notes). Early in my teens, I began to be asked to lead the congregation in singing from time to time. Area Churches also used to have afternoon signings from 2 to 4 pm Sunday afternoons. Grandpa and I would often attend these. I would lead singing for these gatherings. Sometimes, I would take a group of singers that I had got together and directed.

I really loved music and loved popular music of the day in my teen years. It was the Big Band era - Bing Crosby, Frank Sinatra, Nat King Cole, etc. I listened to them all the time. I would, imitate them, getting as close as I could to sounding exactly like they sounded. I memorized all their songs. In my late teens I tested myself and found that I could sing over 300 songs from memory.

When I was about to start Senior High School, the elite chorus was the *a-cappella choir*, but the rule was, you had to be in the boys or girls choir in 10th grade, and if you were good enough, you might be selected for *a-cappella* once you got to the 11th and 12th grades. I, of course, did not want to wait a year. I went to protest to the director of the *a-cappella choir*, and she said she did sometimes consider sophomores through auditions. So I auditioned. After she heard me sing she said if I would sing second tenor I was in. So I did. I also auditioned and got into an elite small group of male singers from within the *a-cappella choir*, called the Mastersingers. I also got accepted into a mixed group, called the *Madrigal Singers*. I learned a lot of great music those three years and became a good sight-reader of round notes. We always memorized music we performed.

One day our Madrigal Singers went to sing for the Lion's Club in downtown Austin. We all walked from school to town, sang our program, and as we walked as a group back to school, we decided to go through the State Capital building. After entering the rotunda area, we decided to go up to the 3rd floor, spread out and stand surrounding the 3rd-floor balcony and sing the program we had sung at the Lion's Club (we did so because we liked the great sound caused by the great rotunda. People came out of offices throughout the building in droves to hear us sing. It was a most marvelous and memorable experience I never forgot.

RED DRAGON PLAYERS

I was in several activities in high school. I was in "The Red Dragon Players," a drama club.

The Red Dragon Players put on a couple of plays each year. I managed to be in all of them. I was elected to an office in the Red Dragon Players, and you can find a picture of the officers of the club in one of my school yearbooks.

The choral department put on a lot of programs. I worked on the school newspaper and wrote my own newspaper column. I was nominated "most popular boy" each year, but never came close to being selected. There were over 3,000 students in our high school. It was the largest in the state.

I was a very popular student and tried very hard to greet every student by name as I walked through the halls each day.

Senior high school was a wonderful time for me and great fun. I had many friends, especially boys with great sense of humor. We loved to laugh at each other's jokes and antics.

I collected lots of 4-part harmony wedding music, formed a chorus' from church members, taught them to sing wedding music, and we sang for lots of weddings. I even sang solos for several. I've sung THE LORD'S PRAYER in a great many weddings throughout my life – even in a few weddings of my children which I also officiated the wedding itself.

No art teacher I ever had in school ever ventured to try to teach me anything about art. I did whatever I wanted in whatever medium I wanted. All my teachers treated me as though I was the best artist in school. Other art students treated me as though I was the best artist, and other students did as well. I won a lot of art contests. It is no wonder I had such an ego. I believed I could become an opera singer for the Met if I wanted to, or I could be a commercial artist... whichever I wished to pursue I was sure I could do it, and there was no doubt in my mind.

The years between the time I was 12, and the time I was 16 are not very clear in my mind, because I was so busy having fun. I dated as many different girls as I possibly could... virtually a different one every week. It was seldom I would have a "steady," and they did not last very long. I would only choose a girl as my "steady" if she was a member of the church of Christ. I would never think of getting serious with a girl who was not.

My best friend for much of my teen years was a boy whose father was an elder as was my father. We were virtually inseparable until one day at about age 16 I realized that he was leading me away from the church and into sin. I immediately severed my friendship with him. After that, my closes friends were of different denominations.

One day, I was to meet one of my best friends (a member of the Christian church) on a certain street corner between his house and mine. I reached the corner first, and he was not yet in sight. In a few moments, I saw him turn a corner onto the street we were to meet. He was several blocks away. I watched him walk toward me. His image got larger and larger as he approached. He finally walked right up before me until we were eye to eye, and he shouted, "**BOO!**" I nearly jumped out of my skin. He nearly scared the life out of me. His name was Gene Plummer and he was in A-

Cappella choir and all the other groups of singers with me. He also sang in his church choir. He invited me to attend his choir practices with him at his church. I loved to sing so much that I began singing with them. It wasn't long until his choir director offered to pay me to sing regularly in their choir at all services. I declined, but Gene and I had many discussions regarding instrumental music in worship. I was never able to convert him.

Another closer friend was Tommy Whiddon. He lived very close to me, just around the corner from our house. He was a Baptist and his father was a deacon in their church. I also tried to convert Tommy, but never did.

One time, Tommy and his father invited me to attend a revival meeting their church was having, so I went one weeknight. I had never been to any denominational church service (except one time I attended a funeral service in a Roman Catholic church). It was strange to me to hear a piano and a choir in a worship service. Even when the congregation sang along with the choir, the piano accompanied the singing. I did not sing or attempt to participate in their service. I was just an observer. When the evangelist offered his "invitation," Tommy and his dad tried to get me to respond, but I would not. Other people made an effort to get guests to respond. The result was that one man responded desiring to put his membership in that church, and right then, they had a vote of the congregation to accept him as a member.

After that service, Tommy's dad took us to have ice cream. Their preacher also came with us and tried to convert me to the Baptist church. It was quite a discussion.
I recall trying to teach their preacher about true Biblical baptism using Jesus' words about being born of the water and the Spirit. The preacher told me that the water Jesus spoke of was not really water but was only a way to speak of human birth, and that one was really born of the Spirit upon

41

their faith in Jesus Christ. I asked him if Jesus had meant water, what other word would he have used? He had no answer and gave up trying to convert me.

The year I expected to graduate, I learned that I lacked ½ a credit to graduate, but instead of graduating in summer school, I decided to stay over till fall, get my credits and graduate in January 1949 at mid-term. In the fall, I took a cappella choir and art, and I doubled in Journalism. I was through with school each day about noon, so I would go to Texas University and play ping pong till I went home in time for supper. I became very good at ping pong entering a competition at the Austin Athletic Club. I placed 3rd in both singles and doubles. That final semester was great fun.
  Journalism was the greatest for me to learn how to write very well. I was always an A student in English (especially grammar) and creative writing. But there was nothing like Journalism to give me writing skill that would greatly benefit me the rest of my life.

I am sure that "Nanny." My grandmother's mother died at 92. After that, my grandma and grandpa moved away, I believe to Los Alamos, NM, and dad bought his house, for we continued living there. I remember we rented out a room to a young married couple. Dad later built a nice garage apartment at the back of the driveway. It was rented to the young couple after she became pregnant. Then later, I remember our living in it.

Through my teen years, my mother seemed to have complete confidence and trust in me. I would get up some mornings in the summertime and ride off without telling mother where I was going, or what I planned to do, or when I would be home. She trusted me completely. I could ride my bike all over Austin, without fear. In all my life, I have never gotten into trouble. I always tried to do what was right, and I always tried to be a good person. When I would come home, mother never asked where I had been or what I had been doing. I knew she trusted me, and I never betrayed that trust. I also wanted to be sure the Norman name was never defamed by anything I did. Austin, Texas was a safe place to live if you knew the areas of town to avoid. Even as a small boy, several of us could go to the city park, just 3 blocks from grandpa's house. It had a great swimming pool that was free. It had a lifeguard, and a deep end and a shallow end. I wasn't very old when I began to go alone. I learned to swim there.

We often went to Barton Springs, but the spring water was too cold for me. We also swam in a pool called Deep Eddy. I painted a pen-and-ink with watercolor of Deep Eddy in art class at school once. It won a school art contest. I was never surprised to win first prize at any art contests; I expected to win (I had great ego).

When dad taught me to drive, he impressed me with dangers of driving. I understood that at all times I must be the master of the automobile – I must always be in absolute control of the car. I must never drive in such a way that the car is not in my control. Consequently, I have never in my life "cut up" in a car and driven recklessly.

The Northside church grew, to the point it had to have two services. We soon built a really nice new building, and by the time I was 16, (and dad was one of the elders) the elders asked me to be the regular song-leader for the church (it had 500 members by that time). The elders said that of all the possible song-leaders in the congregation, I was by far the best. I was to be paid $10.00 a week. In 1945, that was very good money.

Dad was also the Personnel Director of the bank he worked for (The Capital National Bank), and he got me a job each summer of high school, working in the bank. I have no idea what the bank paid me, but I was rolling in dough in those days. I decided I wanted to take voice lessons, so I searched around Austin, and that year, at age 16, I started taking voice lessons from the best teacher in Austin, Texas.

When I was still in high school, and at the age of 17, my mother gave birth to a baby girl. She was the cutest little thing, brown as a berry, and full of life. She turned out to be a handful to raise, but mother and dad were up to the task, and did a great job. The difference in our ages was so great, and my getting married at age 20 gave us virtually no time to know each other, so we have never had a real close brother and sister relationship. Bert, however was a different story. Pat (her name was Patsy Louise Norman) and Bert were very close. She learned the Deaf Sign Language, became fluent in it, and Certified as an interpreter for the deaf.

ANOTHER ART CONTEST

My senior year in high school, I entered a national art contest and won 3rd place in watercolor out of 260,000 entries. It was sponsored by Scholastic Magazine.

The picture I painted does not exist anymore, but in one of my high school annuals, there is a photo of me, my art teacher, some other students, and hanging on the wall behind us is that painting that won that contest. It is a painting of a tug boat in rough water. Actually, it was painted in tempera paint, a kind of watercolor.

After graduating High School, my voice teacher insisted I sing in a recital. I prepared to sing 3 songs. Sometime after that, I was offered a 4-yr. scholarship in voice at Texas University. It turned out some department head had attended the recital. The offer to attend Texas University scared me to death. I said no thank you. I knew I would have to work hard to major in voice, but I would not have to work at all at being an artist (what an ego). My plan was to go to UT in the fall, and major in commercial art.

SCHOLASTIC MAGAZINES

Certificate of Merit

FOR ACHIEVEMENT IN ART

presented to

Dick Norman

whose entry was awarded

Third Prize • Group II

Water Color

In the National High School Art Exhibition, Fine
Arts Galleries, Carnegie Institute, Pittsburgh

MY CERTIFICATE

45

Chapter 4

When I grow up...
I want to be a gospel preacher...

In about 1946, our congregation hired a new preacher His name was H. I. Taylor. I was a paid song leader when he came, and sat, of course, on the front seat so I could get in the pulpit quickly to lead the invitation song. As I said before, our congregation had grown to over 500 members.

H.I. was the most dynamic preacher I had ever heard. Every time he preached I believed he was preaching to me only. How did he know what was going on in my head and life? He seemed to turn me every way but loose.

So, by the time I turned 19, I decided I wanted to learn how to preach. I asked H. I. how I could learn to preach. He said there was only one way, and that was to throw your hat down and start preaching. Then, H. I. told me of Sandy Creek, a small country church with 10 or 12 ladies and one old man. There, I had to do it all; lead singing, lead prayers, serve communion, and preach. I preached there Sunday afternoons at 2 P.M. I was terrible for some time, but I stuck with it, determined to learn to preach. I felt I must, that I had no choice in the matter. Souls were being lost and it was my personal responsibility to do all I could to save them.

H. I. suggested I buy 2 books of sermons written by a well-known gospel preacher named Leroy Brownlow. These books were a wonderful help to me, and I used those books for many years to help me learn to preach and to prepare good sermons.

I still have all those early sermons I preached. Every sermon was written out in longhand word for word. They are in my bookshelf in six 5"X7" loose-leaf notebooks.

H. I. Taylor was my first mentor in preaching. I learned much from him that helped me through the years. For example, he often said, "The Bible is either true or it is not true. If it is true we must obey it, but if it is not true, throw it out a window and live any way you want." That caused me to make a very serious decision in my7 life.

He also gave me many sermon and teaching outlines which I used the rest of my life.

When I was born, there were only two Bibles in the English language, the King James Version of 1611 (which has been updated many times) and the American Standard Version of 1901 (it was said to be "strong in Greek, but weak in English"). Because of attempting to make the American Standard Version truer to the Greek words, it caused the English to be so convoluted that it was difficult to read or memorize. Some years later, I tried to use it in my preaching and teaching, but did not like it at all, and returned to my King James Version. It was in the early 1950s before a new version was produced, the Revised Standard Version (which most preachers rejected out of hand as inaccurate and misleading). I was about 30 years old when the RSV came along, and I did not like it at all, and continued with the KJV for a great many years.

That first church never paid me anything, so it wasn't a career change for me at all. I was still a banker.

Chapter 5

When I grow up...
I want to be a Banker...

Late in July of 1949, after the morning worship at Northside, out on the front lawn under a tree, I saw the most beautiful girl I had ever seen in my life. I had never seen her before and did not think I would ever see her again. Sunday night, however, she was back and sitting with a friend of mine. I decided I would sit with them, so I could meet this girl. After church, I invited them to my house for cokes and to listen to records. I played some Mario Lanza records, some other opera recordings, some Bing Crosby and Frank Sinatra records, and I sang a few songs. Jo and I had a great time and fell in love, but that night, we had no opportunity to be alone together to tell each other how we felt. I learned that her name was Jo Ann Crawford. She was from Cameron, Texas. She was in Austin, attending summer school, and was staying with an uncle and his family. She had come to church that night with Dick Lyle, and Dick Lyle took her back to her uncle's house, but her uncle said all she could talk about that night was Dick Norman.

The second time we were together was on Wednesday night at church. She came alone. Her uncle had dropped her off for church, so I asked if I could take her home, so I could find out where she was living. She said, yes. We had our first opportunity to talk alone for a short time. I went in and met her uncle and his family. Was that a date?

The third time was a surprise to her because it was an unscheduled date. I just dropped in. She was studying, and her hair was up in curlers. Neither of us was aware of the curlers at all. They seemed natural, so I just stayed a while and visited. Then we went out for a ride in the car, and I sang love songs to her. I tried to kiss her goodnight, but she considers that her first "date" with me and said she did not kiss on a first date. I guess this was our first date.

The fourth time we were together was truly a date (our second). We went to a city park to play tennis. Neither of us were very good, so we stopped and sat on a park bench and talked. I suspect it was this date that we expressed our love for each other. It may have been sooner, but I'm sure we were very serious by now and assumed we would marry. We kissed quite a lot.

I am really not sure about which date we did what, but I believe our fifth time together, we went swimming at the local park pool. She was so pretty. She had the most golden suntan, and I noticed (of all things) that she had the prettiest little feet. Many times, when people get old, their feet become gnarled and ugly, but Jo's feet were just as pretty and perfectly formed when she got old as they were when we met. I think that is remarkable. That evening, we again drove up into the hills that surround Austin, and found a beautiful spot overlooking one of the six large lakes on the Colorado River above Austin. I drew her portrait in pastel. It hangs on the wall in my bedroom now.

Our 6th time together was on a Friday. I took her up on Mount Bonnell overlooking lake Austin. It was there that I formally asked Jo to marry me. I presented her with a half-caret solitary diamond engagement ring. She would not accept it. She said she would have to ask her patents if she could accept the ring, but she certainly wanted to marry me. I never spent a dime on her on dates. It was only our 6th time to be together in 10 days.

We had a few more dates, but all were just to be together to talk. On the next Sunday afternoon, I took her to the Lagoona Glora Art Museum. On our ride we listened to opera music on my dad's car radio. The car was a four-door

Chevrolet sedan. It was remarkable that she loved the same kind of music I did. We had much in common. Both of our

Lagoona Glora Art Museum in Austin, Texas

families went back four generations in the American Restoration Movement. In some ways, of course, we hardly knew each other, but we had talked so much in our times together that we both knew exactly what we would be getting into to marry.

She was 17 and only in the 11th grade, and I was 19. I had graduated high school in January (mid-term) of 1949 and was working full time the bank with my dad.

Jo went home to Cameron, Texas to ask her parents if she could accept her engagement ring. We wrote to each other every day we were apart. Her first letter to me had a wallet-size photo like her photo below. On the back of her picture she wrote the words of Ruth to her mother-in-law in Ruth

51

1:16-17, *"Entreat me not to leave you or to refrain from following after you. For where you go I will go, and where you live I will live; your people shall be my people and your God my God. Where you die I will die, and there will I be buried. The Lord do so to me and more so if ought but death part you and me."* She never failed to be perfectly true to those words.

Jo Age 17

When she returned to Cameron, she stayed until her mother made her wedding dress. Jo's two older sisters had married that same year (1049), and her mother had made their dresses.

Her dad told her she could not live with her uncle in Austin and finish high school there. She was to return home or get married. We decided to go ahead and get married.

Jo had the most beautiful golden suntan, and her skin was flawlessly perfect. She had no hair on her arms or on her legs. She never shaved her legs in her life. She was part American Indian. Her great grandmother on her mother's side was a full-blooded American Indian.

Come to find out, our families knew each other, and had known each other for years. They were members of our congregation. In fact, her great-grandfather was not only a church of Christ preacher, but was **one of the 25 preachers my grandfather knew in 1900 that helped evangelize Texas.** He is the one who married a full-blooded American Indian. His name was John Crittenden.

I turned 20 a week before our wedding on September 22, 1949. We were just kids and not really ready for marriage. My grandpa married us. My little sister was our Flower Girl. After my grandma died years later, I performed grandpa's second marriage.

JO'S INDIAN GREAT-GRANDMOTHER,
MADDIE (SMART) CRITTENDON

SNAPSHOT OF OUR WEDDING BY TOMMY WHIDDON'S FATHER

Tommy Whiddon was my best man, and this is our only wedding picture. Jo's aunt had a professional photography business in Austin. She had taken all our wedding pictures, but before she could develop our pictures, her studio burned down destroying all our pictures.

Our wedding:

I arranged for my second-best friend to sing two songs in our wedding, ALWAYS and OH PROMISE ME. I had trained a small group of singers to hum his background music and to sing THE WEDDING MARCH (HERE COMES THE BRIDE) and also THE RECESSIONAL. But the singers had car trouble and were half an hour late. I was so panicked that I almost sang the music myself.

This is a picture of the Cameron church of Christ we married in, but years later it was torn down and replaced by a new church building.

The church where we were married.

It was very hot that day and Jo had to wait before the wedding up in the bell-tower of the church building. By the time our wedding started, she was wilted.

After our wedding reception, we left on our honeymoon. As we drove away, I told Jo that I had never asked if she could cook. She said, "I guess so, I've been cooking since I was 8 years old." Boy was she a great cook! I gained 40 pounds our first year. I told her, "Anybody that cooks like you deserves a fat husband." She never determined whether that was or wasn't a compliment, but I meant it as a compliment.

TAKEN BY A SIDEWALK PHOTOGRAPHER

(Jo was pregnant with our first child. I was seeing her off on a bus to Cameron for a visit with her parents. She was 18, I was 20.)

We went to Galveston, Texas for a weekend honeymoon. Later on our trip, I was kidding around with her about marrying her for her money. She opened her purse and found a dime.

After our honeymoon, we lived with my parents while looked for a place of our own. I had my job at the bank where my dad worked, and upon my getting married, I was given a raise to $100.00 per month. Of course, the church was still paying me $10.00 a week to lead singing. We thought we could live on that, but I had no clue how to manage money, and spent it like it grew on trees.

We found a little apartment, and moved in. I still went to Sandy Creek church and preach, but they paid me nothing. Jo said she was so embarrassed by my poor preaching ability that if she could have found a little hole in the floor, she would have crawled into it. She tried to get me to be satisfied with being a song leader and not try to be a preacher. I, however, was undaunted, and said that I would get the hang of preaching pretty soon. So I stuck with it. It took me about 5 years to get a good "hang" on preaching.

Later, Jo met my mother's dad (my maternal grandpa Waters). He was a very big man. She could place her whole hand in his palm.

Jo's teeth were so bad that she had them all pulled except six front bottom teeth and wore dentures the rest of her life. She was only 19 years old. She never had any problems with wearing dentures. Hers had razor blades imbedded in her side teeth. She loved her new teeth because she could eat and chew anything. It never bothered me that she wore dentures, in fact I rarely ever thought about it.

One day after we had married, Jo was sitting with a small group of young ladies about her age, and they were discussing stockings. They were talking about the color and shades of stockings, and one of the girls said, "I just love the shade Jo is wearing." Jo said, "I'm not wearing stockings. I'm bare legged."

Jo's dad had wanted to name her after the movie star, Joan Crawford, but he was so ignorant of spelling, he fouled it up so that her name is actually Joe Anne Crawford. I called her Jodie most of the time, and she always wrote her name Jo, not Joe.

I continued to work in the bank, lead singing, and preach on occasion... but not for long. I hated banking. Actually, I never "got a job" in banking. Dad got me jobs in banking.

Life for me became a desperate scramble to try to make a living. I don't recall how long we lived at a place, nor in what order. I know I worked in banks until 1954. So, in that five

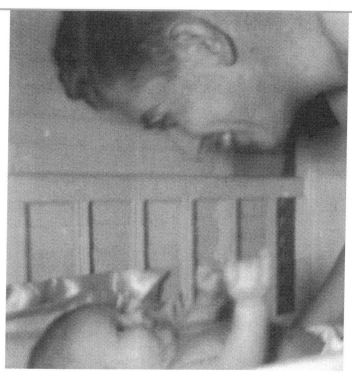

year period, a lot of things happened that I can't unscramble. I had a hard time paying rent, and we had to move in with my folks almost every other month for the first year or so of our marriage.

Jo continued to grow after we married. It scared me to death. I was afraid she would grow to be taller than I. She grew from 5' to 5'4" and stopped. I was 5'7" and maybe a little more, so I was happy she did not grow any taller.

Jo had two older sisters, Jean, who was two years her senior, and Dorothy, who was four years her senior. She also had a younger brother, Charles. Jo and both her sisters married the same year. I don't know how her mother did it, but she did. All three daughters had a big church wedding.

De Dion-Bouton Motor Tricycle

When I lost my song-leading job, I sought more preaching appointments. I also got a night job delivering prescriptions on a 3-wheel motorcycle.

Chapter 6
When I grow up...
I want to be a preacher...
No, a banker...

A three-month tenure in Beeville, Texas.

At some point in this 5-year period, I decided to be a
preacher full time (that tells you about my self-confidence, or
ego). I had no training - no one taught me how to prepare a
sermon or how to do the work of a preacher. However, I
tried out with a little church in Beeville, Texas, and low and
behold, they hired me. The little church had about 100
members, 3 elders and some deacons. Evidently, I had
gotten the hang of preaching a bit because I taught the
auditorium class and preached both services. They were
very happy with my preaching ability. *I got a job preaching.*
I did it myself. I bluffed my way into a job. I had bluffed the
elders into hireling me.

After I got the job, it was a real scramble for me to get up two
sermons every week, and study for two classes. I did not
have any idea how much money to ask for, and so I accepted
too little to live on. I lasted only 3 months in preaching and
had to look for another job. (I learned a lot about preaching
in those 3 months.)

I think it was this point I went to the other bank in Austin.
Dad helped me get that job, but I did not last long at that
bank. I was fired from that bank, but dad was able to get me
a job in a little tiny bank in Bishop, Texas.

Bishop, Texas was a little tiny town in south Texas. I
worked for that very small bank for a few months. At cotton
season, every cotton farmer sent his foremen to the bank

with a big check (several thousand dollars each). We had to cash those checks, breaking them down with a certain number of 100.00s, 50.00s, 20.00s, 10.00s, 5.00s, and 1.00s, so that the foremen would have the exact bills to pay each cotton picker. I would get a check for 3, 4, 5, thousand and various amounts and a list of how they wanted the check broken down. The little bank lobby was jam packed with foremen with checks, and there was a mob outside waiting to get in. There were 5 teller windows, so the bank Cashier and the President helped to fill every window. The Federal Reserve sent us brand new bills. They were almost impossible to separate. We cashed checks all day for 3 days.
My money drawer came up 3 or 4 thousand short. Bank insurance saved me. Needless to say, I did not want to see another cotton season.

Dad then helped me get a job with a bank in Houston. One day in Houston, I was having lunch at the bank and there was a commotion at a window next to my work station. We were on the second floor, and there was a crowd looking out the window. I went to look, and we were looking down at a city bus stopped at the curb. The bus driver was being carried off the bus. He was dead. He had been stabbed.
Later that evening, I was listening to the news on the radio, and they said that the police had been called to an apartment because there was a black man living with a white woman. The police knocked on their door, and when the black man answered the door, he thought they were there to arrest him for the murder of the bus driver, and he confessed. In those days in Texas it was against the law for blacks and whites to live together.

Jo was having a lot of back problems. It was while we were living in Houston that Jo's back went out, and she had a nervous breakdown. She had to have a spinal fusion – hers was the first ever done in Texas. I didn't make any money to speak of at the bank, and the cost of her sugary was enormous. My dad arranged for a remarkable loan for me, and we three moved to Cameron, Texas, Jo's home town.

TEX IN CAMERON AS A CHILD

In Cameron, I got a job as a bookkeeper for the largest insurance agency in town. I struggled to learn to be a bookkeeper. In those days, it was all still done by hand in big ledgers. I hated that job more than any I ever had, so after about three months, I was working very late and made a drastic decision. I laid down my pen, locked up and went to Jo's mother's home, told Jo I quit my job and I took a bus to my parent's home in Austin. There, my dad got me a job in the largest bank in Dallas. It was the best move we ever made.

Our move to Dallas...

Jo felt she did not need her mother's help by then, so we moved to Dallas. It was 1952.

I finally made enough money to live on - barely. In Dallas, we went to church at Skillman Ave., the largest church of Christ in Dallas (1400 members). When we moved to Dallas, I never had asthma or hay fever any more. I had had asthma and hay-fever terribly bad all my life. It was amazing that it just miraculously stopped when we moved to Dallas.

SKILLMAN AVENUE CHURCH OF CHRIST

We put our membership in the Skillman Avenue church of Christ, and I told John Banister, the preacher, that I was a preacher and song leader and I was looking for opportunities to preach and/or lead singing. So, John kept me busy.

The first time he called me he said there was a church that had split over some church doctrinal problems and could I go preach for them and try to solve their problems and help them until they can find another preacher. I preached for them 6 or 8 months. We managed to recover many of their members, solve their doctrinal problems, and help them recover peace and find a permanent preacher.

John kept finding me places to preach where I helped churches that were having doctrinal problems. I became a kind of expert at solving church problems though I was only 22 years old and had only three years' experience trying to preach.

When we moved to Dallas, we lived in a large apartment complex. When Jo would go out in the play yard to call for Richie to come in, another little boy named Richie would always show up first. It made our Richie mad. One day, our Richie came in from play, and announced, "My name's not Richie anymore." It happened that I was at home at the time. Jo said, "It's not? What is it?" He said, "It's Tex." He never answered to any other name again. He was only three years old. He'd changed his own name, and it stuck. We had no problem with his choice, and he has been Tex ever since.

Tex was the most handsome little boy I had ever seen when he was born. He had beautiful black hair, a perfect face, and was precious. I don't remember where we were, but I recall we went into a room full of people one day, and Tex announced to them all, "My name is Tex, and I'm funnier than my daddy." And believe me he was. One hot afternoon, we stopped for gas, and I went in to get us some cold drinks (our car was not air conditioned). I called back out to Tex and Jo, "What do y'all want to drink?" Tex poked his head out of the car window, and loudly proclaimed, "A bottle of Pearl, please." **Embarrassed the life out of Jo and me.**

Another time, just Tex and I were going somewhere in the car together. He was standing up in the seat beside me. We were going down a brand-new street that had just been finished. It was white concrete with curbs and sidewalks. It was beautiful, and spic and span. There was not a mark on it. I called his attention to it, and he asked, "Daddy, why did they build this new street?" Just to be facetious, I said, "So they could tear it up and put some big pipes under it." It wasn't a week later until that was exactly what was being done to that street.

It was at Skillman Avenue church of Christ that I met and became friends with a young man named Newell Oler.

Jo and I and Tex met Newell and his family (I don't recall his family's' names) at the Skillman Avenue church of Christ, where we were all members. Newell had been "first runner-up" to Van Cliburn in the Tchaikovsky Piano competition in Moscow. If Newell had won, he would have had the career Van Cliburn had. That is how good Newell was. I was absolutely in awe of his incredible talent and ability. We became great friends. He was the greatest pianist I ever met. There was nothing he could not play.' He loved my singing voice and often played for me when I sang.

We performed one time for a fancy dinner in the newly built STATLER-HILTON HOTEL for church of Christ graduating seniors in the Dallas area. It was organized for the purpose of giving the young people an alternative to their school proms.

I made a CD of the songs, but the CD got damaged over the years. Tex took lessons from Newell for a while, but Newell was too emotional, too undependable, and we could not keep the relationship going.

I think it was about somewhere in this point in my life, after Newell and I became friends, that I wrote a love song to Jo. It appears on the next couple of pages, and after it is a Christmas song I wrote at that time. I wrote the words and music (harmony- chords) for both songs when I was about 21 and did not ask anybody how.

I did a lot of preaching and song leading in Dallas and, as you can tell, I was not much of a breadwinner in the early years. I lived in frantic desperation, trying to find a way to make a living for my little family. In Austin, somehow, I took two courses in The American Institute of Banking and passed.

In 1952, I worked for the First National Bank in Dallas a couple of years. Little did I know, but I had it made there if I had just stayed with it and applied myself. I moved up quickly. I began filing checks in a vault. About two months later, I was promoted to supervisor of a department with 27 women and one young man. In a few months, I was moved to the Executive Loan Department and placed in charge of the Collateral Department. At the end of my first year with the bank, my boss met with me and told me how much of a raise I was getting. I don't even remember what I was making or how much my raise was. I only recall being incensed. More than that, I was infuriated. I called Jo and told her what had happened and how I felt. She asked me what I was going to do. I said I didn't know. I said I had 5 years' experience in banks, I had started at $100.00 a month, and now was only making (whatever – I think it was only about $375.00 a month, but I am not sure). I told her I'll never make anything in banking. (Here comes another example of my self-confidence and ego.) It was about 10:00 am. I could never have made a living for my family as a painter of pictures, but I found a Dallas Morning News and turned to the want ads. Texas Instruments had an ad for a Technical Illustrator. I had no idea what a Technical Illustrator did, but I knew that an illustrator would be drawing something.

Piano

NEVER IN THIS WORLD

Richard Norman

NEVER IN THIS WORLD

ne - ver hoped to meet you I ne - ver dreamed you'd say a - ny - thing to

thrill me and make me feel this way Ne-ver in this world did I think you would

be mine a - lone to love through-out all e - ter - ni - ty. Ne-ver in this

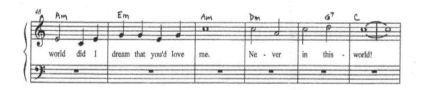

world did I dream that you'd love me. Ne - ver in this - world!

HAVE AN OLD-FASHIONED CHRISTMAS

Richard Norman
words & music

I have a Chris - tmas wish for e - very one to - day, of days gone by

less filled with care. And so to you I say. Have an old - fash - ioned Chris - tmas sprin - kled with

snow. With hol - ly and a Chris - tmas tree lit by can - dle glow. Have an old - fash -

ioned Christ - mas warmed by the ties of old friends and fa - mi - ly and chil - dren's

72

[Title]

star - ry eyes. Mis - tle - toe and sleigh - rides and a yule log bur - ning bright.

make a Chris - mas mer - ry and fill us with de - light. Have an old - fash - ioned Chris - tmas

as an - gels a - bove sing of good - will to all men, and peace and joy and love.

Chapter 7

When I grow up...
I want to be a commercial
artist!

I called and made an appointment for 3pm. I went out to TI
by bus. I met with the head of their Illustration Department
and others in their Employment Department, and told them I
had no education in art, nor did I have any experience in art,
but that I could draw anything I could see. They wanted to
see something I had done, so the next day, I brought the
charcoal drawing I did of Ingrid Bergman as Joan of Arc
back in high school, and a couple of oil paintings and some
other drawings. They hired me as a "trainee" at $1.50 an
hour, but I could work all the overtime I wanted.

Again, I found my own job without my dad's help. Not only
that, but I bluffed Texas Instruments into hiring me. A year
later, I was a Lead Illustrator.

**My very first project at Texas Instruments as a
commercial artist...**

My very first morning at TI, I was shown my station where I would work. I had a huge draftsman's table. In the center drawer under the drawing board, there were a lot of drawing instruments, many of which I had never laid eyes on before and had no idea how to use. My supervisor showed me how all the drawing instruments worked.

Then, they brought me a big piece of art. It was about 4' wide and 15" tall. It was covered with the most complicated wiring design I had ever seen. All the lines were extremely thin and delicate. It was covered with wires going everywhere. My job was to take one of the drawing instruments I had never seen before, and with a lettering guide, letter the wiring numbers next to each of those tiny lines (the letters were also tiny to be able to fit in the available space). It was a job that would obviously take me several days, if not more than a week, working lots of overtime.

Believe it or not, I finished that job, and did a good job. That wiring diagram was a photostat of the original drawing, pasted to a piece of illustration board, so I picked it up, and set it on end, leaning against the wall behind me. I picked up my next big piece of art, which was almost exactly like the one I had just finished and placed it on my drawing board. I took a deep breath and took a step back to look at what I had to do next, and the heel of my right shoe kicked the bottom of the piece of art I had just completed, and the whole thing scooted back against the wall behind me and slipped down through a crack between the wall and the floor, and down onto the sludge below. There was a sonar tank behind me, and a little space between the wall and floor. My supervisor had to get another photostat made from the original drawing I had destroyed, and I had to do the whole thing again.

For months and months, I never saw Tex awake except on Sundays and Wednesday nights. I went to work before he woke up and came home after he went to asleep. There were many nights I did not go home at all. For the first time in my life I began to make enough money to just barely get by.

Then John Banister got me a part-time preaching job with a church... I don't remember what I was paid, but it sure helped. I preached there for about 6 months until they hired a full-time preacher. Then John sent me to a large church needing a song leader. They hired me as a part-time song-leader and preacher. Their preacher was often away, and I preached quite a lot. I don't remember what they paid me, but I am sure it was pretty good for a part-time position. I was with them about 5 years. That church grew so large we had two morning worship services. We soon built a new big building on Military Parkway, and that church was referred to as the Military Parkway church of Christ.

I used Texas Instruments as a school. I absorbed every detail about commercial art. I asked questions of all suppliers like printing companies and art supply companies, etc. I learned everything I could learn about commercial art from Texas Instruments that was possible as fast as I could. Not only was I able to do the work, my drawings were superior to the other artists, especially in regard to special art and design projects. At the end of my first year, I was a Lead Illustrator. At the end of my second year, I headed a new Special Arts Section. My group did all kinds of special art projects for Texas Instruments like color 35mm slides, cover designs in full color for what they called Proposals, and special three-dimensional line illustrations in pen and ink.

I was extremely busy in the 50s. I think that is why I can't remember much. I was always busy with church. I was leading singing or preaching; I taught adult Bible classes Sundays and Wednesday nights (I had to study, you know, and I was still in my early 20s), working very long hours at T.I. In addition to that, I took three courses at SMU (two nights a week), and Bob (my cousin, an interior decorator) got me to do several mural jobs in full color. I also did many copies of oil paintings because Bob did not want to pay the price of the oil paintings. My copies would be much cheaper, and I was able to paint virtually exact copies. I did many other things because I was finding more and more freelance work.

You may recall that my grandfather performed our wedding when Jo and I married. And you may recall my grandmother died. It was not many years after her death that my grandpa found a woman who he had proposed to before meeting my grandmother, but she refused him. He and this old girlfriend began seeing each other, and when he asked her to marry him, she accepted. They were in their 80s. I performed my grandfather's wedding. Turnabout is fair play they say.

While working at TI, a new magazine came into being called "CA", or "The Journal of Commercial Art." I subscribed and took it for many years.

Tim was born in 1956 in Dallas. We named him Tim after Jo's dad, whose name was Tim, and we named him Timothy Wray (Wray, not Ray) after a friend of mine in high school. I just liked the name Wray. I was working at TI. Tim was a big baby. In fact, he turned out to be our biggest baby at 9 lbs. 10½ ounces. He grew tall very quickly, and long before he was school-age, sales people would come to our door, and Tim would beat Jo to the door. The salesperson would ask him why he was not in school. When he was full grown, however, he was not so tall. He grew to only 5'10". Tim was born in October.

Two years later, John came along. We named John after my favorite uncle, uncle Jack, whose name was actually, John Lamar. He was born December 19, 1958. We brought him home from the hospital and laid him under the Christmas tree. He was cuddly as a little teddy bear.

Jo's dad, Tim Armstrong Crawford, died of a sudden heart attack in 1958. He was at his work in his small café' in Cameron, Texas, when he just collapsed and died. All his children from a previous marriage, and his current marriage to Jo's mother gathered for the funeral in Cameron, and all agreed unanimously that Jo's mother inherit all Tim's assets. It was remarkable that there were no family disagreements about that. Jo's dad was 26 years older than her mom. I think Tim Crawford was most fond of Tex because he knew him longest.

The great expense of having more children, and supporting a larger family, of course, put me under a lot more pressure to make more income. I think I was making about $100.00 a week at the church, but Texas Instruments never paid much the whole time I worked for them. It seems like I may have

gotten a $.12 cent an hour raise one time. They gave us a raise every six month, but most of my raises, as I recall, were .03 cents an hour. I don't think I ever made $2.50 an hour the whole time I worked for TI. I found out it was because I did not have a college degree. I had reached the top of my career as an artist at TI (all the other artists had college degrees – one who worked for me had a Master of Art degree. I was the only artist that did not have a college degree.

At some point, I needed a third job. I had already started casting about for freelance work in 1955. I found out that the going hourly rate for freelance art was $10.00 an hour. In those days, that was a lot of money. I began finding freelance jobs. I began making some good money and was building a very nice portfolio. I was getting to know art studios, ad agencies and other sources of artwork.

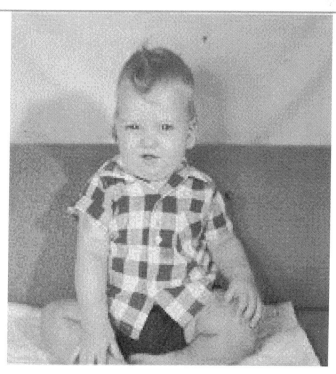

JOHN

My cousin, Bob Henry was an Interior Decorator. He now had his own business. Bob was not successful in his own business. He was *extremely* successful. He got me several jobs.

He had a client that wanted several unusual oil paintings by a currently "hot" Hawaiian painter. His client could not afford the paintings, so Bob asked me if I could do copies of them for "X" number of dollars. Bob had the originals that I could copy from. I jumped at the job. I needed the money. You could hardly tell the difference between mine and the originals. I made several copies of them for myself. Bob had me make one copy for him (an 8"X10"), and over the years I made more copies, giving many away as gifts. I gave one or two to my daughter Carol which she sill has, and I gave one to my cousin, Ruthie which she still has hanging over her bed.

A new Country Club was being built in North Dallas, and Bob was doing the interior decorating. He asked me to paint a large mural on the wall of one of the rooms.

Another time, Bob was decorating the house of a very rich man in Fort Worth, and the man's wife wanted some hand painted decorations done on the ceiling and around the top of every wall as a border of her kitchen and pantry. Jo helped me do that job. We drove to Fort Worth almost every night for more than a month.

Beside the jobs Bob gave me, I found other freelance work, causing me to be incredibly busy in the 1950s, but I learned a lot about commercial art. TI was not worth working for any more. They did not pay enough.

I was just about ready to bail out of T.I. I knew I could do anything the other artists in Dallas were doing. I was building a reputation outside of T.I. as a commercial artist. I was creative, fast, and versatile. I could do just about anything anyone wanted. Without one day of training or experience, I had bluffed my way into my first job in commercial art at TI by telling them I could draw anything I could see (and I could). My art talent and ability is a God given gift. I deserve no credit for it at all.

One day, I got a phone call from a man in Abilene that I did not know but knew of. He was coming to Dallas and wanted to visit with me about a possible job offer.

It was 1958. I was still employed at T.I when the call came from a man I knew as a church of Christ preacher that appeared on national radio and television program called **The Herald of Truth**. He came to Dallas to visit with me.

We met the next day, and he explained that he had stepped down from appearing on the radio and TV programs, to be replaced by another preacher, so that he could promote the programs through an ad agency that he had formed in Abilene, Texas. He was president of the ad agency, and he said they had other clients than The Herald of Truth, and they were seeking other clients as they were trying to build the ad agency in Abilene. He offered me a job with the agency as the Art Director. He offered me a salary I felt we could probably live on without part-time jobs. I don't remember how much it was.

I could foresee problems. I knew of a freelance artist in Abilene who had been doing all the artwork for **The Herald of Truth** since its beginning. I asked why they didn't hire him. He said they had offered him the job, but he turned it down. I also knew they were close friends.

To make a long story short, I took the job. It was the worst decision I ever made.

Our move to Abilene, Texas...

There is no need to tell a lot about our move to Abilene. We bought our first house. It was awful. It was not air-conditioned. It had a water cooler on top of the house. To cool the house, we were supposed to open all the windows just a crack (about 2"). There was no grass, so the water cooler sucked red dirt into the house. Jo would mop and mop, and smear red dirt around on the floor. She would just sit down and cry because she could not clean her house. It was just a little cracker box.

HERALD OF **T**RUTH

His Word for His World. Every Day.™

My first day on the job, I learned that the freelance artist in Abilene changed his mind and took the job as Art Director. I was just an artist, and would work for the Art Director, Jody Boren. My pay didn't change, but Jody Boren was paid much more than I was. There were more than 40 employees.

I could not believe it. Over time, I learned that not one of the employees of the ad agency had ever had one day's experience working in an ad agency before. They were milking **The Herald of Truth** to support the agency as they floundered around looking for other clients.

Jody, the Art Director, had never worked in an ad agency. His experience was at Hallmark Cards. He was good at that stuff. He could hand letter beautifully and do very pretty watercolor scenes. Jody could draw very nicely, he was a fair designer, but his design work looked Hallmarkish.

Needless to say, he expected me to be able to do what he did. Of course I could not do anything he could do, so he belittled me. We shared the same office space, and he loved country music which he played on his radio every day all day. I hated that. We did not get along. I did not fit in anywhere. I could see the agency did not know what it was doing, nor how to do things. I had never worked in an agency, but I had done lots of work for agencies in Dallas, and I had been in them and seen how they operated and did things. Anyway, I decided right away I had made a terrible mistake, and I began trying to find a job back in Dallas. I made trips each weekend as I could, but the way I was treated in Abilene, I wasn't sure I had sense enough to pump gas.

Bob Henry, my cousin, the Interior Decorator in Dallas, had a younger sister, Ruthie, who was married to Lane Cubstead. (They're still living and are in their 80s at this writing.)

Lane Cubstead

Lane worked at the ad agency as a copy writer. He had
never worked for a real ad agency either. Lane, however,
had a college degree and was very capable as a writer. Jo
and I were very close to Lane and Ruthie. They were near
our age, and we had a lot in common. They had two kids, a
boy, Mark, and a daughter, Mary Catherine. One Friday
evening in Abilene, the four of us got baby sitters, and went
out to dinner and a movie. We saw the first showing in
Abilene of Alfred Hitchcock's, "Psycho." Needless to say, we
were all blown away. It made a deep impression on all of us.

The next morning, Saturday, I was going to Dallas on one of
my trips to try to find a job. I don't remember why, but Jo
was going with me, and Lane and Ruthie were also going

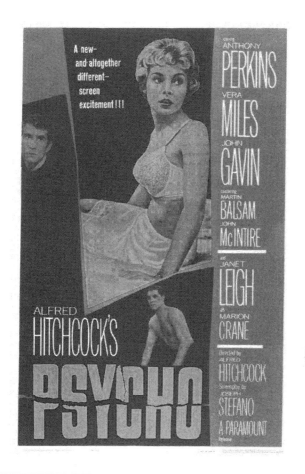

with us. I don't know what it was all about, but I remember
that we had a really good time, and a lot of fun. We left
Dallas after church on Sunday night to drive back to
Abilene. Lane was driving his car, and we were still in the
glow of our good time in Dallas, laughing and joking. Lane
said he needed gas and would have to stop at the next
station. In those days, the highway between Dallas and
Abilene was narrow, and there were few service stations
along the way. It was before self-serve stations. It was a
dark night, and no moon. Ruthie said, "I think I see one up
ahead." Sure enough, we came upon a small, run-down,
station with a couple of pumps, and a small shack for an

office. Behind the shack-office was an old, bedraggled-looking house-trailer. The whole place was dirty, and poorly lighted. We all knew it might be several miles to the next station, and it might not be much better if any. So we drove in. Lane got out to stretch his legs and walk around. A filthy, scraggly, skinny guy came out of the shack to wait on us. He started pumping our gas.

Ruthie got out of the car. She walked about a bit, and then she came over to talk to me. I was in the front passenger seat and had my window down. Ruthie leaned in and whisper-talked to me so as not to let the gas attendant hear. She said, "I wonder if he lives way out here all by himself." I said, "No. He lives with his invalid mother in the house-

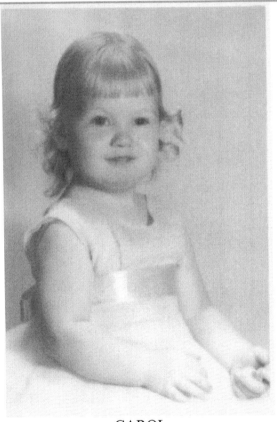

CAROL

trailer in back of the shack." Her eyes got as big as saucers, and she said, "Let's get out of here as fast as we can." She thought of the movie, "Psycho," and it scared the life out of her. (It is all in the timing.)

One night when we tried to take the whole family to a drive-in-theater to see Fantasia, John started crying and acting-up, and began throwing a temper-tantrum to end all temper-tantrums. Jo could not get control of him, so she made us all go home immediately and miss seeing the movie. When we drove in the driveway and stopped, John was still going strong. Jo took him into the house and straight into the bathroom. She set John in the bathtub and quickly turned on the shower with cold water, drenching John fully dressed. He immediately stopped crying for the very cold shower took his breath away.

John never gave us any trouble the rest of his life. As he was growing up, if he began to misbehave, all Jo had to do was ask him if he wanted a cold shower, and he would straighten up immediately, and say, "No."

Carol loved to watch TV. She especially liked to watch a TV show she called "Dick and Dike" (the Dick Van Dyke show), and "Petticoat Johnson" (a TV show called Petticoat Junction). Carol was the cutest little girl, and Jo and I loved her very dearly.

It took me a year to find a job in Dallas. When those in Abilene got through with me I was not sure I could find any kind of a job in Dallas. According to them, I had no sense, and no skills.

Our move back to Dallas...

However, I did find a job with a small manufacturing company in Garland. They had a Technical Publications Department. I was hired to supervise their Technical Illustrators. There were three illustrators besides me. They had three Technical Writers. I don't remember how much they paid, but we seemed to get by on it for a while. It seems they were just starting a Technical Publications Department and were beginning to revise an Illustrated Parts Breakdown book. It was called an IPB. The book already existed, and this company was revising the equipment, and therefore updating the IPB book. We illustrators revised the drawings to show the changes and new parts added or revised. Writers had to update the words. It was a big book... over 1,000 pages. Almost every page had art that had to be revised and copy that had to be re-written. It was a very big job.

A few weeks later, I saw that they had just hired a Technical Writer I knew from TI. He was being interviewed. It was beyond my belief, but he was hired to be Director of Publications. I wouldn't say he was a complete idiot - he was more of an incomplete idiot. I knew him to be totally incompetent and always wondered how he got a job with Texas Instruments.

He and I had separate offices side by side. It wasn't long until he began coming to me to ask for help with his work as a writer. I helped him out so much that after a few weeks, he was fired, and I was put in as Director of Publications. Not too surprisingly, money did not come with the promotion.

That's a little simplistic, but not much. I worked there two years. In that time, I joined the group of commercial advertising artists in Dallas that met for lunch once a month. They reassured me that I did know what I was doing in the art business, and that I could find plenty of freelance work. So I began finding freelance art on the side.

My parents still lived in Austin at this time, and so did my cousin Ruth Ann Cubstead's parents. One time, I don't remember when, my family went to Austin to visit my parents. It so happened that Lane and Ruthie Cubstead and their son Mark, who was about 5 or 6, also went to Austin from Abilene to visit Ruthie's parents.

One day our son, John and Ruthie's son Mark, both about the same age, were visiting together at Ruthie's parent's house. Ruthie and her mother decided to go out to lunch at this "high-end" restaurant and take Mark and John. It was one of those quiet places where everyone seems to whisper, and you hear every slight tinkle of glasses and utensils. Little Mark had this high pitched, glass-shattering voice, and it suddenly burst out in full volume, "LOOK AT THAT BLACK MAN, MOTHER!!" Ruthie was shocked, and tried to calm Mark down by saying softly, "Markie, don't talk so loud." To which Mark replied very loudly, "HE SURE IS BLACK!!" Ruthie and her mother said they were afraid they were going to get their heads cut off. Others in the restaurant tried to ignore the incident. I thought it was hilarious.

Unknown time –

At some point in time, I don't remember when, I got my first job as an Art Director with a real ad agency in Dallas. It was, Evans Young Wyatt (One guy: not three). One of the art jobs I did there was to design 14 billboards that featured a cartoon "granny" in a furniture store. The billboards were all around Dallas. I did not work for him even a year.

When we got back to Dallas, I took my portfolio to go looking for a job. I started on a Monday morning and called on ad agencies and art studios. By Wednesday morning, I told Jo I had over $1,000 worth of work to do by Friday, and if I got a job with an ad agency as Art Director, I would not make anywhere near that much a month. What do I need a job for? I think I'll just freelance again. So I did.

I think it was also sometime in this period that we moved, and one of the movers asked me if I wanted him to set up the swing set in the backyard. I asked him what it would cost me for him to do it. He said $5.00. I said I would do it myself and save $5.00. Later, as I was putting up the swing set, it collapsed on me, and my little finger got caught and was nearly pinched in two. It was broken, but no skin was broken. Jo took me to the hospital emergency, and they said it had to be operated on. The next morning, I realized I had several freelance jobs that were due in a couple of days, and my right hand was bandaged so there was no way I could do any art work. When Jo came in to see me, I was in a panic. She said she would bring the jobs to me; I could explain what to do, and she would go home and do them. After some discussion, she did them. It was the first time in our marriage I learned she had as much art talent as I had. She said she had been watching me work, and figured she could do that, and she could. What a girl I married.

I went to The Abilene Christian College Bible Lectureship. I often attended this annual event. I was visiting with a group of men who were discussing a proposed debate. A man had written a book, **God is Dead**. A prominent church of Christ preacher and professor of Bible at Harding College (then) wanted to debate him about his book. One of the group said he did not see how a man could debate anyone about a book that has not been published yet. He said, "How can you debate about a book you have never read?" I thought, how can you defend a book you have never read... the Bible. The Bible has been a big part of my life since my grandmother began reading it to me every day as a small child. I have read *in* it all my life as I studied my Sunday school lessons, and then started trying to preach. But I had never read it like a novel - straight through, and I was almost, but not, a daily Bible reader. There might be some passages in the Bible I missed, I mean, if you haven't read it front to back, how could you be sure?

So it was 1964 that I determined to be a daily Bible reader and that I would start at Genesis and finish at Revelation and I would read 10 pages every day. I found I could easily read 10 pages a day in well under an hour each morning. I began having my "quiet hour" from 5am to 6am each morning. I learned that by reading ten pages a day, I could read three Bibles a year. I have read three Bibles a year since 1964. I also decided that I would read all the different English versions I could.

(By the way, a few months after moving back to Dallas from Abilene, I heard that Abilene ad agency folded.)

Back in Dallas, Jo became pregnant with twins. It was 1964. We had three boys and a girl, so we were hoping for two girls, to even out the number. No such luck. We had two more boys, identical Twins, Jim, and Joe. I said, "When boys start coming two at a time, it's time to quit." After the twins were born, Jo had a hysterectomy, but the surgeon left her ovaries in place. (She died of ovarian cancer at age 78.) I've often wondered if she could have lived a much longer life if that surgeon had also removed her ovaries.

(And, by the way, four of our five sons take after their mother as part Indian; they have little facial hair, and don't need to shave every day.)

JOE ON THE LEFT, JIM ON THE RIGHT

Chapter 8

I was raised in a White World...

The Integration Movement began in 1955, when I was working at Texas Instruments. In 1955, I was 26 years old.

I was born and raised in a white world. My world was very segregated from the time I was born until I was grown, married, and had a family. All white people were racially prejudiced in those days so far as I knew. It was just the way things were when I was growing up. Everybody used the "N_____" word all the time without thought that it was in any way derogatory. I never went to school with a black person from first grade through high school. I never saw a black person in a public restroom, or in a restaurant, or in a theater, or in a grocery store, or in a department store, or in a public park, or in a swimming pool. I remember seeing drinking fountains for "colored," and restrooms for "colored." Blacks sat at the back of trolleys and buses. On sidewalks in town, blacks moved aside for whites. Some white people treated black people terribly bad. They talked ugly to them, daring them to talk back and give them an excuse to hurt them or kill them. In spite of being a Christian family, we were not without guilt of discrimination. I became a Christian at the age of 12. I recall black Christians visiting our white congregation when we had a gospel meeting. When I saw them I realized they were Christians just as I was, and I wondered why we did not all meet together. It was the first time I thought that something was not quite right. I also began to realize we lived in a very segregated world. As time went on, and the great Desegregation movement began, I was greatly disturbed. I was afraid segregation was so entrenched, that it would take another civil war to end it, a war between the blacks and the whites

93

this time. I could not imagine blacks eating in a restaurant with white people. I could not picture in my mind a white waitress taking a food order from a black family. I just could not see integration actually happening in schools. I certainly could not conceive of intermarrying with any other race, even Mexican, or Asian.

I remember the sit-ins, the marches, the confrontations with police and blacks. I remember, of course, the killing of Martin Luther King, and all that went on in the integration years. It was amazing to me that the transition was made as smoothly as it was. It wasn't perfect by any standard, and it is still a work in progress. I must admit that it was not easy for me, but as a Christian, I knew it was the right thing to do, and I had to become unprejudiced. It was easier for Jo than for me. She was a much finer Christian than I. It was so ingrained in me, I still have to work on myself all the time.

Chapter 9

About my paintings...

MY THIRD ART CONTEST
My very first oil painting was "the Sampan," and it won
honorable mention in an art exhibit at the Dallas Museum of
Fine Arts. I can't remember the year.

THE SAMPAN

I did a good amount of oil painting from 1950 to 1959. I had
never painted with oils until after I married, and we had our
first child. My parents had allowed me to subscribe to
American Artist magazine when I was about 16 or so. I

devoured every issue. I often went to Laguna Gloria Art museum IN Austin, and the Dallas Museum of Art when we moved there. I joined the Texas Fine Arts Association when I turned 18. It cost $5.00 a year. (I don't know why I joined.) After I married, even making extra money outside of my banking job, it was still a struggle to live on what I was making, but I continued taking American Artist, and kept my membership in the Texas Fine Art Association. I don't remember the year, but I do remember we were living in a very cute little duplex next door to the head coach of the Texas University Longhorn football team. I talked to Jo about spending money on painting supplies, and she encouraged me to go ahead, that we would work it out somehow. I promised to be as frugal as possible, and I was. I got the very minimum of supplies I felt I had to have to paint in oils.

I began casting about for something to paint. I have never been good at painting or drawing from imagination or memory. I have always said I can draw anything I can see. I don't recall what I chose, but I made two attempts on a couple of canvas boards I had bought. I was very disappointed in both of them and destroyed them. I went back to looking for something to paint. Jo helped me look. We looked through magazines, books, and whatever else we could find that had pictures in it. Charles, Jo's younger brother, had just gotten out of the Navy, and had sent her a big book like a school annual or some such thing. It had pictures all through it. Jo was looking through it, and suddenly said, "Here it is!" She showed me a full page photo of a Japanese Sampan (it is like a Chinese Junk). It was a beautiful photo, but it was in black and white, not color. I said I couldn't paint that because it was not in color. She said, "Why not? You can paint it in color." I said I can't paint it in color, I can't see it in color." She said, "Sure you can, just try it. I believe you can."

Jo never did anything but encourage me in everything.

We continued to look for something else. We looked for about a week, and during that time, I kept going back to the Sampan, and studying it. Finally, I said I would give it a try.

I have no idea how long it took me to paint the sky, the mountain and the Sampan, but I was completely stumped when I got to the water. I worked on the water, and it looked terrible... it did not go with the rest of the painting. I would give up and try again another night. This went on for several days until one night I began fooling with it, and I began to see it coming. I yelled, "It's coming." I could not stop, I was afraid I would lose the color I had and would never be able to find it again. It was 2am when I finished. I had to be up at 6am to go to work at TI..

When I got home the next day from work, I took a look at my first finished oil painting, and said, "Oh, no." Jo said, "What?" I said the water was not in perspective. She looked again, and said, "I see that. Can you fix it?" I said I could try. I had painted the water so that it came toward us too flat. It was not in proper perspective. The nearest edge of the water was about two inches above the bottom edge of the canvas. I did not get it fixed as long as we were living in Austin.

After we moved to Dallas, in 1952, it was not until 1957 until I finally got the water in the right perspective (that is the date I put on the painting as being finished).

I think it was about 1958, that I got a notice in the mail that the Dallas Museum of Art was going to have a show featuring the Texas Fine Arts Association artists, and they were calling for entries. Since I was still a member, I was invited to enter one painting. I think by that time I had several paintings I could choose from, but I felt my Sampan was the best I had. Jo and I took it to the Dallas Museum of Art and we entered it. There were 750 entries, but they could hang only 75 paintings. My Sampan won Honorable Mention. Jo and I went to the show, and I looked at the paintings that won first, second and third place, and I was incensed that I did not win first place. I thought my Sampan was far better than any of those others (my great ego again).

MY FOURTH ART CONTEST

Later, I got a notice of a show in Austin, at Laguna Gloria. I had painted an abstract picture, on Masonite, of ships in a harbor. I had used painting knives. I do not remember painting it. I don't remember when or where I painted it. I'm sure Jo would remember all about it.

THIS PAINTING DID NOT MAKE OUR MOVE TO
MILWAUKEE, WISCONSIN IN 1964

I feel certain the painting was done in Dallas. I also believe it took me only a couple of hours or so to paint it. Bob thought it was too long and needed to be cut off about 3" or 4" on each side. I sawed the painting off on each side. It looked terrible to me, so I glued the ends back on and retouched where they were cut.

I entered the harbor painting, and it won second place. They said they wanted it to go as a part of a traveling art show that would travel around the United States for a year. That is about all I can remember about that painting. One of our children has it now, Tex I believe.

THE HARBOR

After we had moved to Dallas, and I was working at the bank, and one day, I was walking down the street on my lunch break. As I was passing a jewelry store, I stopped to read a sign in the window. It was an announcement of a "BUSINESS MEN IN ART SHOW." I went inside to learn more about it, and learned that the owner, Mr. Evert, was a "Sunday" (amateur) painter. He wanted a platform to show his work and thought there were other businessmen who might also be amateur painters and would like to show their work. So he decided to have an annual show in his store and invite all Dallas business men to enter. I asked if I qualified, and I did and so I entered a painting. It was not a competition. I entered every year as long as Mr. Evert lived. Evert's Jewelers was the largest Jewelry store in Dallas. When Mr. Evert died, the store went out of business.

I don't remember what I painted or when during those years. I do remember one year I did not have a picture to enter in the "Business Men In Art" show at Evert's Jewelers. I went by the store and told Mr. Evert I was not going to enter that year, and he said I had entered every year from the beginning, and he couldn't have the show without me. The deadline was the next day. I went home that evening, found a picture of Venice that was a double-page spread in a magazine. I painted it with painting knives that night. The next day, I took it wet to be framed, and then to the store to be hung wet.

Painting was not a major part of my activity. It was more work than enjoyment for me. I certainly did not think much of art contests. I could not imagine an art contest with entries like Van Gogh and Rembrandt against each other. It's silly. However, I won 1st, 2nd, 3rd, or Honorable Mention in virtually every art contest I ever entered until I was 70. I didn't enter any after I was 25, and only entered about 8 or 10 paintings in shows at most.

Chapter 10

Commercial Artist! No Wait, Preacher! Uh, Welllllll?

I think it is important to note again that I was 8 years old when I decided I wanted to become a commercial artist, and I did. And, at TI, I quickly reached the point that to advance, I would have to change my career... there was no place to advance as an artist; I would have to become an engineer or something. The same thing was true at the little company I worked for in Garland. As a freelance artist, I was free to make as much as I could handle, limited by the going hourly rate of the time.

I do not remember why I decided to try full-time preaching and move to Beeville. There had been times in my late teens and early twenties that I had considered being a preacher instead of an artist. I had also considered trying to become an Opera singer. Getting married pretty well ended that pursuit.

The church and the Bible had always been the center of my family's (the Norman's) life, and Jo and I were trying to do the same in our life. Before we married, a preacher counseled us, "There is no problem that can arise in a marriage that two Christians can't work out together." We tried to live by that premise.

In 1965, we attended a world missionary workshop at the Webb Chapel church of Christ where we were attending. My father was one of the elders there. I was deeply moved to be a part of that effort. It was the same one I told about earlier that grandpa said he would do that if he was younger.

Anyway, back to our decision to go into a mission work. We talked about it at home as a family, and the few of our six children that seemed to understand, approved of my decision.

When I made known my willingness to go to some mission work the next day, I had several choices. I decided it would not be practical to haul six children overseas, then not be able to adjust to the culture shock and cause the expense of bringing us back overseas. I felt we ought to find a work that was in the US.

Chapter 11

When I grow up...
I want to be a missionary...

Grandpa had said to me one time, **"Don't be a preacher if you can help it."** I did not understand why he would say such a thing at the time, or exactly what he meant. Now, I did. There is only one reason a man wants to preach: **Because he believes souls are lost, and he wants to try to save them, and they can only be saved by the gospel of Christ. There is no other reason to preach.** It certainly isn't for the money. I could always make more money in a week without trying very hard as a commercial artist than I could make in a month as a preacher.

We move to Milwaukee, Wisconsin...
I was to preach for the church at 35th & Cherry. It was 1965. Consider my qualifications to be a preacher. The only

college education I had was 9 hours at SMU. I had Freshman English 1 & 2, and Speech. Up until 1964, I had done quite a bit of preaching part-time. Sometimes I had preached for several months at one church. We lived in the Dallas area, and I often attended a preacher's luncheon that met each Friday at Wyatt's cafeteria.

I knew and was known by most all the preachers of churches of Christ in Dallas County. From early in my married life, I subscribed to a monthly publication of a religious paper called, The Firm Foundation. I don't remember when I began sending in religious articles, but everyone I sent in was published, and by 1964, many had been published, and I was noted as a very good writer. The publisher and editor, Ruel Lemmons was a very good friend.

REUEL LEMMONS AND THE FIRM FOUNDATION PAPER

It was 1965 that we moved to Wisconsin. The twins were 9 months old, and Jo had 5 children 7 years old and under. My work there was to be a missionary. Our first meeting with the little church was on a Wednesday night. There were 17 in attendance, and eight of them was our family. I think their membership was about 35 or so. The little congregation could not support us but would pay us what they were able.

To complete our financial support, the largest church of Christ in the world, at that time, provided the rest of my meager income. That was my introduction to the Madison church in Madison, TN, a suburb of Nashville, and to Ira North, their preacher. Ira and I became good friends, and I learned a great deal from him about building a great congregation. All the secrets to their growth were presented in Ira's little book, YOU CAN MARCH FOR THE MASTER, and I devoured that book so that I knew exactly how to help a congregation to grow.

I had no idea how to be a missionary. I had heard many missionaries talk about their work in various countries of the world in the World Mission Forum at Webb Chapel church but learned little that would help me. I had read much about mission work in various papers and books but saw little that seemed would help me in Wisconsin. I had read John Banister's book, "The Work of a Preacher." According to the New Testament, my job was to save lost souls. Actually, I believed, and still do, that Paul's letters to Timothy and Titus tell us what the work of a preacher is. I developed a plan based on those three New Testament books and Ira's book.

First, we tested the neighborhood around the church building. We had a group of preacher students from the Preston Road School of Preaching in Dallas, to come up and knock doors in a ten square block area around our building, offering a free home Bible study. Not only were there no takers, we got a very hostile reception. That wasn't going to work.

105

I was very discouraged. One day I was rummaging around in my home office in the basement of our house and came across a small box with a card file in it. It was left in the desk by the previous preacher. It was full of cards with names and addresses, but little else. I wondered what these names were here for. I got the courage to dial the first number. To make a long story short, these contacts were people who were receptive, and in a short time, I was teaching three and four home Bible studies every week, and I had ten more studies on a waiting list. Some of these were members of the church who had moved to Milwaukee, and were out of duty, and needed to be restored. I began baptizing a few, and new faces began to show up. It was slow, but it was working.

Having *Ira North* come up and preach for us helped.

IRA NORTH

An all-black congregation in Milwaukee was the largest church of Christ in the state of Wisconsin. They had over

300 members. They had a gospel meeting and a very prominent black preacher, Marshall Keeble preached that gospel meeting. He was over 80 years old.

I attended that meeting, met brother Keeble, and invited him to preach his last evening in Milwaukee at the all-white congregation where I preached. He agreed to come.

We invited all churches of Christ in Wisconsin to come to 35th & Cherry to hear brother Keeble. Over 750 people came from all over the state to our little building which could accommodate about 700 people counting our balcony. There was standing room only, and brother Keeble had the smaller children come and sit at his feet around the pulpit. Church members of Wisconsin said they had never seen that many members of the church of Christ in one place before.

MARSHALL KEEBLE

I preach to over 3,000 people...

Our family was invited to the church in Madison for me to preach and give a report on our work in Milwaukee. It was exciting to speak to such a large congregation. One of the elders at Madison kept following me around that day, and often stuffed several &20.00 bills in my pocket secretly. I had well over $200.00 when we left Madison. He also gave us a big Buick Electra, free, and took our trashy Ford wagon as a trade.

I learned so much from my association with Ira North and the Madison elders. I got on their mailing list for their church bulletin. I began taking the religious magazine, The Gospel Advocate. I began writing religious articles that the Gospel Advocate published. I became an avid student of Ira and the Madison church. If anybody knew how to make the church grow, it must be them. I don't remember when Ira North became Editor of The Gospel Advocate, but I submitted many articles for publication the entire time he was Editor, and all were published.

The bottom line, however was that though the work was going well (our congregation was nearing 100 members), as a family, our experience in Wisconsin was a disaster. It was a horrible place to live. Though Jo rose to the occasion to be a great asset as a preacher's wife, she hated the place. Tex had a terrible time, as did all our children. I did not like it either. The people were rude and mean. It was cold year around.

I remember once, Jo had a hard time finding a hair salon that had an opening for an appointment for her to get her hair done. When she got an appointment, she told her hair stylist that she had called ten salons that said they were booked up. Her stylist said that if she had talked with her, she would probably have claimed to be booked up, too. Jo asked why, and the stylist said it was her Texas accent. She said she would have thought she was black. In Wisconsin, they were as racially prejudiced as anybody in the south.

Near Christmas time, I went into a little shop that had lots of unusual, interesting trinkets that I thought I might find an unusual gift for Jo. I moseyed around the store looking at different things when, all of a sudden, the store owner said to me, "What do you want?" I looked at him and said, "I don't know yet. I'm just looking around right now." He said, "If you don't know what you want, get out of my store." I left.

I remember once being downtown, and watching this taxi turn into an ally near where I was standing. The passenger door opened, and a man with one leg struggled to get out. The handicapped man turned to walk away, and the taxi driver yelled, "Hey. You may have one leg, but you have two arms. You shut that %#@* door." He shut the door with his walking stick. That was a perfect illustration of my impression of Milwaukee Wisconsin.

Life in Wisconsin was hard on all our family. Our kids had to walk to and from school, even in the snow. I am not sure, but it seems most of them came home for lunch and went back to school. That meant getting them all in their snow clothes in the morning, getting them out and back in them at noon and out of them when they came home.

Then Jo had to fix breakfast, lunch and dinner for eight of us every day. We could feel a cold breeze blowing across our floors all the time. The twins were nine months old when we moved there, and it seems they were sick the whole two years we were there. Jo got little sleep, tending the twins at night. She often said they slept all night, one at a time. Jo would go out in the middle of the night and shovel our sidewalks. Our kitchen did not have a dishwasher, so Jo had every one of us wash our own dish, and she did the rest. Tex's school was even dangerous. It seemed kids always wanted to fight with Tex. He said, "I don't know about fighting. How about dirty looks at 20 paces." I even got sick once. I got an ear infection and lost my balance. I never get sick - well, hardly ever.

One day I set up a home Bible study with a very nice-looking young couple with two beautiful young children. The husband wanted to be baptized. He had been taught very well, but I learned that his wife was a member of a church of Christ in some southern town. The elders of her home congregation would not baptize him because he'd had a previous marriage and was divorced. The elders told him he would have to divorce his current wife before they would baptize him. I could not believe my ears and told him I would baptize him that evening. I could not see breaking up what I saw was a wonderful and very happy home, tearing it apart for some stupid reason. I believed, and still do, that baptism washes away all previous sins. The husband told me that before he learned the truth he was a wild and wicked man, He often fornicated, and after some time fornicating with a girlfriend (who also had been a frequent fornicator), they married, but after marrying, both committed adultery many times and eventually divorced. I believe the young couple had every right to marry and he needed to be baptized so they could raise their children in a good Christian home. I studied with them several months but could never convince him that he could become a Christian. Those elders will have to account for their sin in his regard. I would not want to face Judgment Day guilty of such ungodliness.

We were all happy to leave Wisconsin and would be happy to never see another snowflake. We had been there 2 years.

Oh, yes, we had not been there a year, when a young man began coming to church. His name was Larry Bertram. After a while, Larry asked to meet with me. I learned that he was a recent convert, and that he wanted my help to get him into the Sunset School of Preaching in Lubbock, Tx. I managed to do that. He said I had inspired him to preach.

I think my children suffered most, especially Tex. Tex had a terrible time at school, and Jo and I took advantage of him at home. I am very sorry, and I apologize for the way he was treated during those years. Jo had a bad time in Wisconsin. It was very hard on her. Still, **I think it was divine**

110

providence that we went to Milwaukee. I was blessed to know and become friends with brother Ira North and have a relationship with the great Madison church. It helped so much in my work in Milwaukee. It was providential that I met and was able to help Larry Bertram become a gospel preacher. I helped him get into the Sunset School of Preaching in Lubbock, Texas. There were many evidences of God's providence in our work in Milwaukee, Wisconsin. The church grew to become self-supporting soon after the next preacher came, and they installed elders and deacons. I did what Paul told Titus to do, "set the church in order, and appoint elders" {Titus 1:5.).

I found a church in Kansas. Some years later, 35th & Cherry merged with the Southside congregation and ceased to exist.

Chapter 12

We move to Kansas...

When we were moving to Kansas from Wisconsin, I was driving the U-Haul, and Jo was driving the car with most of the kids. It was night, and very dark. As we approached the town, I got confused, and made several turns. Jo honked at me to stop. I did, and she came and asked me where I was going. I admitted I was not sure. She said to let her lead. Unknown to me, we had driven around, and were now entering Hutchinson, Kansas from the south, not the north. Therefore, the whole time we lived in that town, I was turned around. Every day, the sun came up in the west and set in the east. When I made trips to Dallas, I almost drove north. Jo had to remind me to head south. One day, I went to see someone who lived on the west side of town and I went east. I never got my directions right.

I was very impressed with such an opportunity; to go from a small mission church to a large church that covered a city block. It had an auditorium that looked like it could seat 500 or more, and an annex for fellowships about the same size as the auditorium. The annex had a huge kitchen, fully equipped with the finest kitchen equipment. They had plenty of Bible rooms. I don't remember how many members they had, but the auditorium was pretty full on Sunday mornings. They had 5 or 6 elders, and lots of deacons. They had a very nice house for their preacher that was just across the street from the church building. I had a nice office and a full-time secretary in an adjoining office. I don't remember the pay, but I must have thought it adequate or I would not have accepted their offer.

The preacher before me had been there for 10 years. He was much loved. No one wanted him to leave. Not even the elders. He was not fired. When he left, it was like a funeral. He could do no wrong. When he preached, he liked to use a big visual aid, felt board. It wasn't long till I was asked if I was going to start using a felt board (they knew I had been an artist). I told them, no, that I thought it would be a big waste of my time to do all that cutting and pasting and designing of a large visual aid for each of my sermons.

Well, that did not go over very well. There were several deacons there that played golf two or three times a week, and they would invite me to play with them. Preachers could play free. My grandpa had given me his old set of clubs. I knew that the previous preacher played golf with them, sometimes two or three times a week. So I went golfing with them about once every other week. I wondered, however, when their previous preacher found time to study if he spent all his time cutting out stuff for his visual-aids and playing golf. It was there I learned to hate golf.

We made the mistake of taking in a foster daughter in
Kansas. She had lived all her life in a dormitory situation
and had never experienced any kind of family life. She was
17, I think – the same age as our oldest son, Tex. We tried
to teach her to fit into family life, but it did not work out at
all. Finally, she found an aunt who would take her in, and
she left.

One day one of the elders told me about a young "kid" (he
called him) who wanted to be a preacher. I don't remember
what all he said about him, but my impression was that the
boy was too young, and he was the village idiot, and not
worth sending to preacher's school. I already had my doubts
about the elders of that congregation, so I invited Roger
Dixon into my office for a visit. I found him not to be a
village idiot, but a very smart young man. He had a high
school diploma and had made pretty good grades. He had
gone to the local community college, and had not only gotten
a degree, but his grades were very good. He was no genius,
but he was certainly no dummy. He wanted to go to Preston
Road School of Preaching in Dallas, so I recommended him.
I was told that mine was the only positive recommendation
Roger got. All the others were negative. It was solely on the
strength of my recommendation that they took him. Roger
made straight A's all the way through Preston Road, and
graduated with honors. He and his wife went into foreign
mission work and are still there as far as I know. Roger has
written and published a number of religious books and
articles. I think it was divine providence that brought us to
Kansas.

It was not very long until I learned at an elder's meeting, that
I was expected to visit in every church member's home (with
my wife) during my first year with the congregation. In that
conversation that evening with the elders, I learned that they
expected me to "Pastor" that church. They did not state that
specifically but implied it in their concept of a preacher's

work. If the Bible is true, and I believe it is, elders are to "pastor" the congregation, not preachers. That is not my job as a preacher according to I Timothy, 2 Timothy, & Titus. It was time to search for another church (I could see I was not going to work this one out). I began my search.

About this time, I heard that the Wisconsin church installed elders and deacons, had a full-time preacher, and were self-supporting.

I could find no churches that would respond to my letters. I talked with Jo about going back to Dallas, and finding a job, perhaps in art again, at least, not in preaching.

I made a trip to Dallas, and found that a large aircraft company, Ling-Temco-Vaught, was hiring Technical Writers. I had done a little of that when I worked with that small company in Garland. Seeing nothing else, I decided to give it a shot. To make a long story short, I talked them into hiring me, paying me a good salary, and paying for our move to Dallas. Again, I bluffed my way into a position I was not really qualified for. I had virtually no experience in technical writing, no degree, and yet was hired.

The very night I got back to Kansas, I got a call from a church in Springfield, Virginia. The elders wanted Jo and me to fly up and interview the very next Sunday. They were having a gospel meeting, and therefore I could not preach Sunday morning or night, but I could teach the auditorium class Sunday morning, and I could preach in the afternoon at 3pm.

I looked up the information about the church (it had advertised "looking for a preacher"). The church had about 200 members and was offering the highest salary for a preacher I had ever seen. We decided we would give it a shot.

We flew out on Saturday, and the airline lost our luggage.
We were to stay with the Himes family. Phil Himes was one of the three elders. We had no change of clothes, nothing to sleep in, nothing to wear Sunday morning. I had no jacket. We slept in our underwear. I was to teach their Sunday morning adult auditorium class. I asked what I should teach. Phil said the class was studying a workbook from the Gospel Advocate, and the lesson for Sunday was on "giving." He gave me a book. I had nothing more to study than the class had and little time to prepare.

Sunday morning, we cleaned up best we could, and put on the clothes we came in, and went to class. I did the best I could, but when worship time came, their guest preacher (they were having a gospel meeting), was an old preacher who knew my grandfather personally. He told the congregation that if Richard Norman was half the man his grandfather, Luther Norman was, you couldn't find a finer preacher. Divine providence was at work again in my behalf.

Right after lunch, the airline found our luggage and delivered it to the Himes' address by taxi in time for us to change before my 3:00 pm preaching time. There was not a very large crowd to hear me preach at 3. Our flight back to Kansas was Monday morning, so we attended the evening worship. My assessment was that I probably did not have a chance with this church. I expected to just go back to Kansas and get a rejection letter in a few days.

I was surprised that the 3 elders wanted to talk to me after the evening service. We met in a small room in the basement. They asked me a few questions, and then offered me the job. They asked me how much money I would need, and I told them the amount they had advertised was good. They said, oh, that was an old figure. We pay more than that, and they made a better offer. I could not believe how much (I don't remember). I also learned I would have an associate minister, Gene Chumley, a retired Army Colonel who had been General Westmoreland's aid in Viet Nam. The next morning, they showed us the big fine house we would live in. Jo and I could not believe we got that preaching job. We flew back to Kansas and began making preparations to move.

First, I had to resign the job I got in Dallas with Ling, Temco, Vought. I called them, and we had a long talk because they were very angry with me.

Chapter 13

We move to Springfield, VA, a suburb of Washington, DC.

I remember the drive to DC. When we reached the Smoky Mountains in Tennessee, we just were breathless at the magnificence and beauty. Then when we got to the Blue Ridge Mountains in Virginia, we were more overwhelmed at the magnificence and beauty. We had never seen such huge mountains before, nor such overwhelming beauty. When we drove up to the house we were going to live in, the twins had been confined so long, they were anxious to jump out of the car and run around. But they kept falling down. Jo said it was due to the ground not being flat in Virginia. We had come from flat country to a very hilly country. The

little kids would have to get used to ground that was not flat.

We moved to Springfield, VA, a suburb of Washington, DC, in 1968. For me, it was the best move I ever made as a preacher. I don't recall how much I was paid, but it was the most I had ever been paid as a preacher. We were provided a very nice big, 2 story house in a very fine neighborhood with beautiful, tall trees, and rolling hills. Northern Virginia is one of the most beautiful areas of America.

The church building was very nice, and in a beautiful wooded area with tall trees. I had a very nice church office, and a very good church secretary who worked full-time for free. Her husband was a high-paid government employee, and she did not need any money. She just wanted something to do while her husband was at work (their children were grown and married). She was very efficient and professional.

The congregation was unique... Most of the members were highly paid government employees; all the three elders were. There were 3 generals in the congregation: 1-Army, 1-Air Force, 1-Marine. We had a Navy Commander, and we had one member that had 2 PhDs. I called him Doctor-Doctor. He thought I was very funny and never objected. Most of the congregation were middle-age, and highly educated. My associate minister was a full Colonel retired and incredibly efficient. There were about 200 members. That was who I had to preach to though I had only 9 hours of college and very little experience preaching, but I had learned much in a short time.

I had talked to the elders about what I wanted to do for the Springfield church. I told them about having the secret to the growth of the Madison church in TN, where Ira North preached, and how it grew from a little church of 45 or 50 members to more than 3,000. I asked if they wanted to try it. They said yes. This was the only church that let me put

119

into motion the things I learned from studying the books and the history of Ira North and the great Madison church. The three elders were the best elders I ever worked with. They knew what elders were to do, and they let me do my job. My associate would do anything I asked, and he was at least twice as fast and efficient than I was. I told him I could never keep up with him. He said not to worry about it, he would not complain. He was great to work with, and we never had a problem.

The first thing I wanted to do was write all of the church bulletin (except for my associate's article) and mail it each week (it had been handed out on Sundays before).

Writing and mailing a bulletin is the only way a preacher can speak to every member every week whether they come to church or not. I could promote every aspect of the programs of the church in a positive tone through the church bulletin.

This was a congregation that was ready and willing to work. With my associate's help, the congregation was organized into (I don't remember how many) visitation groups. **We did our best to visit every visitor, every absentee, and every newcomer every week.**

There were several other things we did, but in 4 years, we had to enlarge our building twice, and begin two morning worship services to handle the attendance. We went from 200 members to over 550. To handle the activity in the church office, we increased to a total of 5 **church secretaries, all unpaid.**

The last year I was there, we hired Larry Bertram, the young man I had helped get into Sunset School of Preaching in Lubbock when we were in Wisconsin. He had married, and the church hired him as our youth minister.

When we went to two worship services, it meant I would speak 5 times on Sundays and 1 time Wednesdays.
 Sundays, I preached at the early service, taught a Bible class, preached again at the second service, then, Sunday evening, I taught a Bible class (we had Bible classes Sunday evenings), and preached Sunday night. And, of course, I taught a Bible class on Wednesday nights.

That took a lot of study and preparation, and a lot of energy. I never thought anything about it. I loved every minute of it.

John was 9, and we were on vacation, visiting Grandmother Crawford in Cameron, TX. He was bored, so he decided he wanted to learn how to play the piano. I knew nothing about this, of course. I was also bored but was reading. John came up to my chair and ask me how to read music.
 Teasingly, I wrote, m-u-s-i-c on a sheet of paper. John was really upset with me, so I quickly drew lines and spaces, notes, and identified the notes on the scale, and put in a treble clef. Then, I did the same for the bass clef. He went away, and I heard him plinking on grandmother's piano.
 From time to time, John would come to me asking about this marking and that marking in music. I just answered his questions briefly. I never tried to sit down with him at the piano and teach him to play. I could not play the piano, but I could read music. Sometimes I would send him to his mother to answer a question. Jo could read piano music better than I could. Jo played the piano a little, but not really well.

A few years later, when we were living in Dallas, I came home on day and heard Jo playing Fur Elise, which she often did. Suddenly, I realized she was playing it better than I had ever heard her play it before. She just could not play it that well, so I went to look, and it was John playing. I knew that was remarkable. It is just absolutely phenomenal. No 9-year-old teaches himself to read classical sheet-music well enough to play Beethoven. I knew he needed piano lessons.

John says that he and Carol and Tim had taking class piano. Tim and Carol dropped out rather soon, but John continued taking piano lessons everywhere we moved. (More of this story later.)

Living in Virginia, 1968 – 1972...

There is one more thing about the church in Springfield, VA that was unique. The attendance in Bible school was often almost the same as the attendance at worship. Sometimes the difference was only 5 or 6 different. One Sunday, it was only one. Most of the time, it was 15 or 20 different. It was remarkable. I have never seen anything like it before or since.

As far as I can tell, it seems to me that our family liked living in Virginia, especially in a suburb of Washington, DC. It was so beautiful and green. The trees were so thick and tall. There was so much history there in Virginia, and DC.

Tim said the schools were terrific; in field trips especially. He mentioned a dozen places in the DC area that he got to see when he was in school. I believe all the kids liked the schools and liked living in Virginia. As a family, I

Van Gogh's *Cornfield and Poppies*

think we tried to visit some of the special places in the area like the Washington National Gallery of Art. Of course, once I had seen it, I tried to go see it every Saturday.

Until then, I don't think I had ever seen any original impressionist paintings. I think I had only seen printed reproductions. Consequently, I had a very low opinion of Van Gogh's works. Printed copies do not do him justice. When I saw Van Gogh's real paintings, I was completely blown away. I could not take it in – not in one viewing. My eyes were not big enough - I could not see enough. I could not stay long enough, I would have to come back, I had no choice.

The same was true of the other impressionists. I had read someone had said, **"You could go blind looking at Van Gogh's corn fields."** Now I could believe it.

Eventually, I saw a Van Eyck's painting, the originator and inventor of oil painting. It was only an 8X10 inches, but it was remarkably realistic, and it looked like it had been painted that morning and the paint was still wet. Oil painting is only about 600 years old.

It seems that in these years, I could not keep busy enough. There was a small Christian college close by, just up in Pennsylvania, and they began offering Bible courses in the Washington, DC area. My elders said I could take classes as I wanted, so I began night classes, and while living in VA, I obtained a good number hours of college credit.

It was while we were living in VA, that Jo got an invitation from Abilene Christian College (then it was not yet a University), to come during the Abilene Christian Lectureships, and present a women's class on "Teaching with Visual Aids." She wrote her book, "Consider the Eye-Gate for Christ," and I illustrated it. We had it printed and sold it when she presented her class. I thought that was pretty good for a little girl who had only finished the 11th grade. Jo was very smart. We didn't break even on her book. We lost money.

We were in Kansas when Tex published his book of poetry, "Reflections In A Tear." As I recall, I think it did pretty well. I remember that I really enjoyed illustrating it for him. Then, when we were in Springfield, Tex was asked by one of his teachers to use his book to teach a class about poetry. I think he was asked to do that same presentation to a class in a different school. I don't think he made much money on the book, but hopefully, Mr. Burson didn't lose any money on it.

[Note: Mr. Richard Burson was the man back in Hutchinson Kansas who paid to have Tex's book published.]

Tex was very smart. He finished high school, and we sent him off to Texas to start school at the Preston Road School of Preaching. He was to stay with my parents in Dallas. I didn't think that would last long, and it didn't, but I was not able, financially, to help him. Somehow, he made his own way. (We sent him off from home, giving him a Gremlin car.)

Tex was greatly missed. We were so used to six children, that when he left, it left quite a HOLE in our family. It was really hard on Jo, especially. Tex was the first to leave the nest, and it really did make a big difference in the family.

As Tex grew up, I remember how smart he was, especially in English. He understood poetry and read a lot. I never understood poetry, and I did not start reading till later in life (I was good in English grammar in school). Because of the gap in years between Tex and his siblings, I am sure he had no idea how much all his siblings were in awe of their big brother.

Through the years Tex has done many remarkable things, and I have been very proud of him. He taught himself to play the guitar and he sang very well. He led singing in church very well. He could really preach well. When he left home to go to school, he never asked for a dime, nor did he ask to come home again to live. I would have helped either way.

Eventually, Tex entered Oklahoma Christian College. I thought it remarkable how he took 15 hours each semester, worked a full time job, and obtained his college degree in three years. It was at OCC that he met and married Kathie. Jo and I did not attend the wedding. It was a small, private affair that was done on campus by one of his professors.

Kathie had severe diabetes, and it was prohibitive for her to have children, so they adopted a precious little newborn boy born January 13, 1979, who they named Ryan. Tex and Kathie were first to present us with a grandson. What a wonder Ryan turned out to be. A precious little boy, you could see it in his eyes. Tex and Kathie did a marvelous job of raising him. He grew up to be a handsome young man, and very smart, in fact, he is a genius. Ryan obtained a PhD. In a remarkably short time from Princeton University and was hired by the school after his graduation to be a research microbiologist. Ryan worked there many years. Jo and I are very proud of him. Tex has a fine family.

Later on, Tex himself built a log house. It was a superhuman effort. Tex is very like his mother in that he seems to be able to do whatever he wants to do. He paints well, and sculptures, and does any kind of art he wants, and does it really great. He has written and published a good number of books as well.

One day in Springfield, Virginia, a preacher came to see me. He preached for a small congregation in McLean, Virginia, a northern suburb of Washington, DC. They had about 150 members. They had not had a baptism in 5 years, and the elders wanted to fire the preacher, but one of the elders was the preacher's father-in-law, and he did not want to fire his daughter's husband or his grandchildren's dad. The preacher did not want to leave right then but wanted to stay until he could bring peace back into the congregation, and then he would resign. The congregation was in turmoil, fussing and fighting. I told him, "Bill, forget about it. Just pack up and move away. The church is resilient, it will survive without you." He would not listen to my advice, so he stayed until he tore that church apart. Several months later, I got a call from a man who had been one of the elders at McLean. He said they had no elders now, and only about 30 members. I had offered to preach them a gospel meeting free of charge, "Building Up The Local Church." They wanted me to do that, so I did. It seemed to help them a lot.

1971 was an important year in my life. That was the year I learned how to paint in oils like the Old Masters. I read some books that told their technique, and I followed it in painting three pictures. I have used the technique of the Old Masters in my paintings ever sense.

Springfield Virginia...

One Sunday morning at the Springfield church, one of the elders was announcing a new birth. The mother's name was Becky Duckworth (funny enough), but he said, "Ducky Beckworth." The congregation laughed, but he had no idea he had mispronounced her name. He frowned and looked around and said, "what? All I said was 'Ducky Beckworth had her baby.'" That broke up the crowd.

Our only true vacation, Cape May, New Jersey...

One day, I can't recall the year, the Magreers invited us to take a weeks' vacation with them to the beach in Cape May, New Jersey, Colonel Magreer said they owned a place on the beach. In my mind, I pictured some small shack of a place, and I was not interested in taking my family of seven (Tex had already left home for college) to be crowded together with the Magreer family of seven (they had five children still at home) in some small shack, so I declined. Eventually I learned that their place on the beach was a big house with plenty of room for all of us, so I accepted their invitation. It was quite a vacation and a most unusual experience for me and my family.

When we arrived at the Magreer's house on the beach, we were overwhelmed by the size of the house, it was enormous! I never counted the bedrooms, but I know Jo and I enjoyed a very large bedroom with a private bathroom and a big very comfortable bed.

The Magreers had also invited another family of four as well. Another man, an Episcopal priest, related to Mr. Magreer, was also living in a small apartment built into the house. Then there was a detached three-car garage apartment

127

behind the house in which a young navy couple rented. They had a small child, a toddler.

All the boys (9 in all) were assigned to sleep downstairs in a very big basement room with several bunk beds. It was quite nice and roomy for all the boys. The girls (3, Donella (the Magreer's daughter, our daughter, Carol, and the other couple's daughter – I can't remember her name or the name of the other couple who, I think, were relatives of the Magreers) were assigned to a big, fine-looking attic room.

The Kitchen was huge and fully equipped. The three wives did all the cooking, and every meal was sumptuous.

We all had a wonderful time. I read some, frolicked on the beach a bit, and walked way out on a jetty made of huge stones. One evening, I fell onto one of the stones and cut my head, but it was a small cut of no consequence.

One evening, Lester and Donna invited Jo and I to a fine restaurant for an expensive lobster dinner. I don't believe Jo and I ever dined finer or in a finer restaurant in our lives, nor did we ever have a more luxurious vacation.

The Revelation...

It was in Springfield that I told a preacher friend that I had become a heretic. He asked me why, and I said it was because I believed I understood the book of Revelation (at that time I had read the Bible about 40 times). I told him I believed it was about the destruction of Jerusalem in AD70, and the fall of the Roman Empire. My friend said, "That's what Foy Wallace believes." I did not know that. I thought I was the only one to believe that. I bought Foy's book; a commentary on the book of Revelation and read it. It pretty well was like my idea about The Revelation letter. (I had led singing when a teenager for a gospel meeting in Austin, Texas when Foy Wallace preached. He was a good friend of my grandfather.)

What I believe the book of Revelation teaches...

1. I believe the book was written around AD 68. The book seems to imply that some apostles were still alive, and if it was written in AD 96 or 98, as many believe, all apostles were dead except John. Also, if it was written in AD 96 or 98, Jerusalem and the Temple were already destroyed by Titus of Rome in AD70, and surely something as significant as that would have been mentioned by John in the book of Revelation.

2. In AD96, secular history records that John was, at that late date, so weak and sickly that he had to be carried about, and he could hardly speak. He would not have been able to write The Revelation.

3. Most importantly, however, Jesus gives us the most positive proof in Matthew 24, where He tells His apostles about the destruction of the Temple and Jerusalem. Jesus tells them that Daniel had received a vision of "the city and the sanctuary" in his day (Dan.9:26). Daniel was so distressed by the vision, he mourned three full weeks (Dan.10:2), and said, "no strength remained in me" (Dan.10:8, see also vss.16-17). Then, Jesus says Daniel refers to his vision as "the abomination of desolation" (Dan.11:3 & 9:26-27).

    Then Jesus tells His apostles *they will see* Jerusalem and the Temple destroyed (Matt.24:15), and Jesus calls it a "great tribulation" (Matt.24:21), and He tells that many Christians will survive (Matt.24:16-22).

    Jesus also tells His apostles about Him "coming on the clouds" (Matt.24:30).

4. In Revelation 1:7, we read of Christ "coming with clouds," and John says he (John) will be "both your brother and companion in *the tribulation*". Then John

says that those in white robes (Rev.7:13), "are the ones who come out of the *great tribulation*" (Rev.7:14) – speaking of surviving Christians just as Jesus did in Matt.24:16-22.

It is Jesus that ties all three passages together, telling us that John is writing in Revelation about the destruction of Jerusalem and the Temple by Titus of Rome in AD70.

Then, later on in Revelation, John writes of the fall of Rome (Rev.18). (That's enough to get you started on the right track.)

I got some schooling in Virginia...

I took a number of courses: Restoration History, New Testament Greek, How We Got The Bible, and a few other courses. I made excellent grades, generally, except in Greek which I only audited.

For some reason, I decided we needed to move back to Texas. I don't think any of the family really wanted to move, just me. Anyway, I found a little church with about 100 members or so that was looking for a preacher. It was in Denison, Texas, just south of the Oklahoma border. I went down for an interview, and was hired, so I went back to Springfield, and resigned. It was probably the worst mistake I ever made, at least it was one of the worst mistakes I ever made.

The church in Springfield was growing. We were at a point where we needed to build a larger building. Our Bible class facility was to capacity, and our auditorium was just about full. We were having to have two morning services. I have always wondered if we could have grown like the Madison church in Madison, TN grew (to 3,000 members). I certainly believe divine providence guided us to Springfield, VA. Phil Himes told me some years later that after I left, the church just dried up.

My final year in Springfield, we baptized just over 100 souls.

Chapter 14

We moved to Denison, Texas

The church had provided us with a very nice Preacher's home in Dennison. It looked like a brand-new house.

The movers did an excellent job of moving us into the house. All the beds were set up and made and ready for us.

It was Wednesday, so we went to church Wednesday night. School was to start the next morning, and some of the kids said they needed a few school supplies. Jo said we needed milk for breakfast, so I decided we would leave the kids at home and Jo and I would go to the store. It was after 9:30, so we had to hurry, because Kroger's closed at 10:00pm.

When we got to the store, we went straight to the back, and picked up a gallon of milk. As we began looking for the school supplies, we started up one aisle, and were met by a skinny black woman with a gun. She ushered Jo and me, and another customer (a woman) to the back of the store. Along the way, I put the milk jug back in the shelf, and positioned my body between Jo and the gun the black woman was holding.

At the back of the store, there were two or three customers and a young male employee already in the custody of a black robber who also had a gun. The black woman wore a mask, the man did not. She turned the three of us in her custody over to the man and went to find some more customers. Again, I positioned my body between Jo and the man's gun. She and I were facing each other. Jo was looking over my shoulder, watching the man with the gun. A young mother with a small baby in her arms said, "I can't believe this is real." The man with the gun said, "I think we ought to shoot one of them to prove it's real." At that precise moment, he was distracted by the skinny black woman bringing more customers to the back. Jo told me later that when the man said he ought to shoot one of us, she saw him point his gun at my back.

They talked about what to do with us. Suddenly, they started herding us into the men's bathroom. It happened so fast that Jo and I were separated. Jo panicked and tried to make her way into the men's bathroom where I already was, but the robbers had already figured out the bathroom was too small to hold all of us, so they started herding us into the meat locker across from the restrooms. The skinny black girl took a stand by the meat locker door and hit every one of us on the head with her gun as we passed her. After Jo and I were in, I could hear them pistol-whipping the young male employee. When he was pushed into the meat locker, he was very bloody. She had conked Jo and I on the head once with her gun, but she hit us really hard, and it really hurt, and our heads really bled a lot. The robbers left us alone in the meat locker. It was cold, but not freezing. Some of the other people in the locker began to suggest we leave. Some wanted to go out the door to the parking lot. Others wanted to go back into the store. I told them we had better just wait for the police to come get us out. About that time the door opened, scaring us all to death. A gray-haired lady was shoved in. She was the night manager of the store. She said that one of the robbers had grabbed her by the hair, pulled her to the safe, and told her she had one chance to open that safe. She was really trembling with fright, but she opened the safe for them.

It really wasn't very long until the police came. They took Jo and me to the hospital where we got stitches in our heads where the black woman had hit us. Then they took us to police headquarters where we looked at mugshots for hours trying to identify the robber that didn't wear a mask (to no avail), then they took us home.

We had called Tim as soon as we could after the police freed us, to tell him where we were, but told him not to tell the other kids. We didn't want them to worry. However, Tim found some big black headlines in a magazine that read, WE'VE BEEN ROBBED! He cut them out and placed them on our bed. We were paranoid for weeks, afraid of virtually every black person we saw wherever we went.

One of the elders stopped by my church office each morning to take me out for coffee at the nearby Dairy Queen. It was poorly managed and so filthy I did not like going there. It was then that I began calling the Dairy Queen the Dirty Queen.

I also had a church secretary. Dennison was a very small country town. The church had scheduled a gospel meeting, so I designed and had printed a flier to distribute throughout the town inviting everyone to attend. When the fliers were printed, I asked my secretary to go to the printers and pick up our fliers. She looked confused and asked why she should go to the printers to pick up the fliers. It took a few moments for me to realize she thought I'd said flowers because that's how she pronounced flowers.

After we had lived in Dennison only three months, I got a long-distance call one evening from a man in McLean, Virginia. He told me that the church there had split and had lost more than half its membership. He reminded me that when I was preaching at Springfield, Virginia, I had preached a gospel meeting for the McLean church. He said the church at McLean wanted me to come and be their preacher. I told him I just could not do that. I told him I had just moved to Dennison 3 months ago and did not feel I could leave a church so soon. We talked a while and hung up.

I pretty well forgot about the phone call, but about a week later, I got another call from them. I was told that the McLean church wanted me to come be their preacher and made me an offer.

They said they had enough money on hand and in the bank to pay me for 3 months. They could also pay for my moving expenses back to the Washington, DC, area, and they had enough to pay my rent and utilities for 3 months. Every member of the McLean church would write to their "home congregation" to ask for support, and thereby raise support for us in three months. Now, the deal was, if I did not agree to come to McLean and be their preacher (accepting their 3-month terms), they would close up the church, disband, and sell the building.

What was I to do? I would have three months security. School had just started. I would have to drag my kids out of school again. They would have to change schools again. I felt that the church had to survive in McLean, VA. What else could I do? We were sure it was God's will. I took the job.

Chapter 15

We move back to Virginia, to McLean, a northern suburb of Washington, DC

As I recall, I think the church at McLean had only about 40 or so members left when we got there. They had no elders or deacons. There were two men who had been elders, and perhaps a few who had been deacons, but none now.

They rented us a fabulous house in a marvelous location. It was a large two-story brick house just a few houses off Georgetown Pike, and near The Beltway. The church building was on Georgetown Pike, across the street from Langley High School. About a mile on down Georgetown Pike was the CIA headquarters at Langley. Georgetown Pike connected George Washington Parkway with The Beltway.

The house was very large and comfortable for us. It had a den in the lower floor, with a fireplace. The rent was paid for 3 months.

The church also had a substantial contingency fund. Each member pledged to write their "home congregations" (virtually everyone in the Washington, DC, area is from some other place). They raised a very substantial amount of support in less than 3 months. I had nothing to worry about in trusting that the Lord would take care of us. I had just jumped out of that airplane without a parachute and landed on my feet. It was divine providence, I'm sure.

I thought the church building was really nice looking. It had the classrooms and fellowship hall downstairs in the basement. I had a really nice office on the ground floor, and an office for a secretary. There was no provision for a secretary for me.

The kids went to Langley High along with the kids of the coach of the Washington Redskins, George Allen. McLean was where the elite people of Washington lived. The Robert Kennedy compound butted up to the church property, for example, and all our members were doing pretty well in order to live there. The church parking lot was filled with the most expensive automobiles of that time.

McLean was a beautiful place to live. My drive from the house to the church building was wonderful. Along Georgetown Pike were large homes way back from the road, and spacious equestrian training farms (I don't know what to call them) on either side of the road. There were lots of tall trees and places where there was thick forest and underbrush. There was a hill that had been cleared by an Episcopal church, and a beautiful building crowned the hill. The church building had a golden dome that blazed every morning in the bright sunlight. They had planted various-colored dogwood trees that covered that hillside, and they kept the grass perfectly clipped when the dogwood bloomed. It was one of the most beautiful sights I have ever seen in my life.

I was in the local Post Office one day to pick up the mail for the church, and a young man came bursting into the building, greeting everyone loudly, bustling around and making noise. I really don't know what all he did, I just know that he sure caught my attention. When he saw me, of course I was looking at him, so he immediately came and introduced himself, shaking my hand. He told me he was something I can't recall, and that he was with the Episcopal church up on the hill and in training to become an Episcopal priest. He was extremely likeable, and he took a liking to me. We became good friends and saw each other mostly at the Post Office. He liked to joke around, and so did I, so we kidded each other and laughed and had some fun.

DOGWOOD BLOOMS

In the mail one day, I got an invitation to his "Ordination Ceremony" to become a priest at the Episcopal Church. I had never had such an invitation before. I was never ordained. I toyed with the idea of going, but I was apprehensive and a little afraid of what I might be getting into. I decided I would ask him about it next time I saw him at the Post Office (his Ordination Ceremony was a month away).

He was there the next day, so I told him I was thinking of attending his Ceremony, but I did not know what to expect, and was not sure I should come since I was not an Episcopalian. He said I did not have to be an Episcopalian. He said anybody could come. He said, "You can even participate in the 'laying on of hands.' We have extra robes, so you can wear one in the Ordination Ceremony. There will be several Pastors of other churches that are going to participate. You won't be the only one."

I told him I had never been ordained, so maybe I was not qualified to ordain someone else. He said that would not disqualify me and he would like to have me participate in his ordination to the priesthood.

I said, "In the churches of Christ, we believe in the priesthood of all believers."

He said, "We do too."

I said, "Yeah. But we practice it."

I went but did not participate. After his ordination, he was assigned somewhere else.

I preached for the McLean church two years. We grew large enough to be self-supporting in the first six months I was there, and they dropped all outside support.

At the end of our second year, I resigned with no visible means of support. We put all our furniture in storage and drove to Dallas. I told Jo that I had a paycheck from the church last Sunday, and the Lord will provide; I will have a pay check from some church next Sunday. I believed I would find a church needing as preacher and get hired so I would not miss a paycheck from one Sunday to the next. And we didn't. Once again, I jumped out of an airplane without a parachute, but divine providence prevailed.

Chapter 16

We move back to the Dallas area, to Grand Prairie

It was **1974**. I preached my final Sunday at McLean, and we rolled into my parent's driveway the next Friday afternoon. Saturday morning, I began calling preachers I knew in Dallas to ask if they knew any churches in the Dallas area that were looking for a preacher. I had made several calls, until I was told by a preacher I knew that a church in Grand Prairie was looking. I made contact there, and, to make a long story short, I was invited to preach at Grand Prairie the next morning. In fact, I was to teach a class and preach Sunday morning, and preach Sunday night. I would meet with the elders and their "search" committee after the evening service. They hired me immediately and paid me my first full check that Sunday just as I had said would happen. I had a job.

On the way out of the building that evening, there was a commotion in the foyer. I learned that a large group of men of the congregation were demanding to meet with the elders immediately, but the elders said they would only meet with them individually, one at a time. I was standing right there when I heard one of the men say, "I think we ought to take these elders out in the parking lot and stomp them into the pavement." I told him, "That is a good Christian attitude."

*Some preachers don't want to take a church with a lot of problems. Some preachers leave churches because they have a lot of problems. Let me tell you: **every church has a lot of problems**. I never preached for or ATTENDED a church that did not have a lot of problems.*

Churches are made up of people, and people have a lot of problems. The Bible teaches that all people are sinners. All people outside the church, and all people inside the church are sinners. Inside the church, we have forgiveness of our sins readily available at all times through prayer, "if we walk in the Light," we have continual cleansing of our sins. A preacher's job is to "set in order the things that are lacking" in the churches (Titus 1:5). In other words, he is to preach to the needs of the church to create "the unity of the spirit in the bond of peace" (Eph.4:3). And, if the church where he is preaching needs elders to oversee the flock of God, the preacher is to see to it that elders are appointed.

So, I accepted that preaching assignment with that congregation, knowing full well what problems they had.

That church's problem was that they had, at that point in time, only two elders to oversee a congregation of somewhere in the neighborhood of 500 members. Also, one of the elders was an older man of about 60 or so, who had only a 3rd grade education. The older man worked in a large aircraft manufacturing plant as a maintenance man. The other elder was younger; in his late 40's. He worked in the same large aircraft manufacturing plant but was an executive. He had a master's degree, and was smart, articulate, and had an outgoing personality. He was energetic and well-liked. The older elder was slow, slow of speech, and shy.

Consequently, a good-number of members felt that the younger elder ran the church, called all the shots, made all the decisions for the congregation, and the older elder, being so uneducated and shy, was just a "yes-man" for the younger elder. They put it this way: "this church has a pope."

To make a long story short, after some time analyzing their problem, getting to know the congregation, and preaching lots of sermons on peace, unity, and other needful subjects, I learned in many meetings with the two elders, that they were both fine elders. They worked together in perfect harmony, and the older elder was every bit as qualified to be an elder as the younger man. Both were well qualified, and the younger elder did not run roughshod over the older elder. The older elder would never have allowed that. The older elder was not a "yes-man."

I told the elders that I believed the way to resolve this issue was to add more elders. I pointed out that I knew there were several good men, well qualified that could serve with them, and resolve the problem. Not entirely, of course, but it would be a beginning.

That is what we did. It took some time and effort, but eventually, we sought out from among the congregation, and went through the process, and added, I think, 5 new elders, and several more deacons as well. We ended up with 7 elders and I don't recall how many deacons. No longer did we have a "pope" running that church.

That did not solve all their problems, but it really helped. There was still some unresolved issues to be dealt with, but I was not to be the one to deal with them.

I got a phone call from a former client of mine when I was a commercial artist in Dallas.

Grand Prairie was a suburb of Dallas. My former art client told me that a friend of his had just been made President of Lubbock Christian College (now University) and was looking for someone to head up the Department of Public Information. My former art client had recommended me.

I told him I could not consider such a job. I had not been at the Grand Prairie church a year yet (probably not much over 6 mo.). I told him I knew nothing about Public Information, I had no college degree in anything, and I would not know anything about working for a college. He said my years of experience as a freelance commercial artist in Dallas was all the experience and education I would need to do the job. He said that the new President of the school was going to call me, and I should at least talk to him.

I got the call from the new president of the school, and I told him all the reasons I had told my client-friend why I could not take such a job, and why I could not leave the church I was preaching for, and on and on. He would not take "no" for an answer and asked me to at least fly up to Lubbock and meet with him about the job.

I flew to Lubbock the next day and was talked into taking the job. I had no business taking that job.

Chapter 17

When I grow up...
I want to be a
Collage Administrator...

I had told the new President of LCC, that I had no clue about being Director of Public Information for the school, but he promised to help me. He didn't. He paid no attention to me whatever. I could not find a Job Description; I could not find a departmental budget; I could find nothing that told me what my job entailed, nor what my department plan for the year was, nor how much money was available to spend on Public Information and advertising that year. I knew nothing about my job or what I was to do. I soon found out that the new president's job was in jeopardy, and he was scrambling to try to save it.

We went to church at Sunset church of Christ, where the
Sunset School of Preaching was located. What a joy. At that
time, Sunset was at its best. Richard Rogers was preaching
at the church and teaching in the school. All their best
teachers of the school of preaching were there. Our first
Wednesday night, Jo and I went to Jim McGuigan's class on
the book of Daniel. The next Wednesday night, I asked Jo if
she wanted to try a different class (other teachers in the
school of preaching were teaching Bible classes on
Wednesday nights), and she said I could go anywhere I
wanted, but she was going to Jim McGuigan's class on
Daniel. We went there, and it was really great.

At noon, I would go to the Sunset church, take a sack lunch,
and eat with Richard Rogers and all the other teachers of the
school. We would discuss difficult Bible verses and argue
with each other about all kinds of stuff. I learned so much.
Richard Rogers was "a preacher's preacher." I could not get
enough of his preaching. It was really great. While we were
there, occasionally I led singing at Sunset, and eventually
taught a Bible class.

All adult classes studied the same lesson each Sunday, so I
was asked to teach next Sunday's lesson to all adult
teachers on Wednesday night before Sunday morning. I did
that for some time.

While I was employed at LCC, I was allowed to test out on
two Bible courses. I passed them both and got 6 hours
college credit.

I also took Evelyn Wood's Speed-reading course (free), and
greatly increased my reading speed. When I began the
course, my speed was 250 words per minute. When I
finished the course, it was in the thousands. Now, I

146

normally read about 500 to 750 words per minute.

One morning, I went into the office of a man who was in charge of fund-raising for the school (I can't recall his title, but it was impressive). After a brief visit, I turned to walk out, and caught my foot in the wire from a wall-plug to a giant coffee machine on a windowsill. I pulled it off, spilling a freshly brewed full pot of coffee across the floor of his office. It was a huge disaster. His floor had to be replaced.

One morning the school president called me into his office. He apologized for never helping me with my job, but he fired me. I was stunned (I don't think it had anything to do with the above incident).

Once again, I had to look for a church that was looking for a preacher. I found one in El Paso and was surprised to learn that one of their elders had visited the church in Grand Prairie. We had met and had a long conversation. He had heard me preach several times. He was anxious for me to come to El Paso. We did and were hired.

Tim, however, had found a girl named Sue, and decided to stay in Lubbock. He got a summer job with LCC, with the expectation of attending college in the fall.

Once again, we had another big hole in our family. We were down from 8 to 6 children. It is really hard when kids grow up and leave the nest.

We had found a very fine piano teacher for John in Lubbock. Though we did not live there very long, John was like a sponge, and learned very much very quickly in Lubbock.

We began making plans to move to El Paso.

Chapter 18

Nah... I think I wanna be a Preacher...

I think we must have moved to Lubbock in winter and lived there about six months or less. We must have moved to El Paso in late Spring or early Summer, and I am not certain of the year. It seems strange, but again, I think the church membership was something like 400 or 500. They had a bus ministry and brought in about 60 to 80 kids on Sunday mornings.

One Sunday morning, a young soldier came forward, wanting to be baptized. I baptized him, and he talked to me a good while after services. I told him that if there was ever anything I could do to help him in any way, come to see me. On his way out of the building, I saw him pick out a bunch of tracts. The soldier's name was, Tom Barton. Over the next couple of weeks, Tom brought a soldier, friend of his that he had taught, to church to baptize him. Tom baptized him. Over several weeks, Tom taught and baptized 15 of his soldier friends. They all came to church regularly.

One night, John saw a car parked out in front of our house (his bedroom had a window facing that way). It was late, but John got up, went out to see who was in the car. (John should be telling this, I'm not sure I have it right.) He found it was Tom sleeping in his car. John brought Tom in, got Jo and me up, and told us Tom had been sleeping in his car out front for several nights. Tom said I told him if he ever needed help to come see me. He said, "So here I am." He said since he became a Christian he could not stand living on base anymore, so he moved back home with his parents. But because he tried to tell them about his conversion, they kicked him out of the house. He said he had nowhere to go.

John said he had room in his room, so we told him to bring in his stuff. Tom became like one of the family. He just fit right in. He was never any problem but was always a great help. The nicest young man you would ever want to know. He said he thought of Jo and me as his mom and dad. We always have thought of Tom as one of ours.

When he got out of the army, he went to the Sunset School of Preaching. When he graduated, he did not become a preacher, but a parole officer. He worked his way to the top of his profession and is now retired.

Tom helped us when we moved back to Dallas, even drove one of the U-Haul trucks. Tom and John were real close, and still are pretty close.

When we moved into our house in El Paso, our next-door neighbors were a young couple. The husband was a doctor, his wife was pregnant, and about to be delivered. I can't remember, but it seems like they had one little boy. Anyway, after we got moved in and settled, the neighbor lady had her baby. It wasn't any time until Jo got real worried about her. I don't remember, but I think the woman had some complications in giving birth, or something, and Jo noticed she had no one coming to help her. So, Jo went to see about her, and sure enough, she was in a mess. She had no help, and she was virtually helpless. Jo just pitched right in and took over. She took care of her baby, took care of the lady, cleaned her house, etc. She continued to come each day to take care of the woman, her baby, and her house. The lady said that no one in her family or her husband's family would lift a finger to help them. She could not believe Jo would do so much for her. Jo told her it was because she was a Christian. She learned that the lady was also a Christian but was out of duty. Her husband, however was not a Christian.
As soon as the lady got well, she and her husband began coming to church. They invited Jo to study with them, and

it wasn't long until she was restored, and I baptized him. They became faithful members at Northside in El Paso. They had a backyard swimming pool, and Jim and Joe learned to swim in it that summer.

At an elder's meeting, we discussed what we might do to help the church to grow. I came up with the idea of having a "BUS PARENT'S APPRECIATION DAY."

We would send our bus kids home with an invitation to their parents to come to church with their children on a certain Sunday, and we would show our appreciation to them, the parents, for their letting their children ride our busses to our church. We would show our appreciation to the parents by having a dinner on the grounds in their honor. Boy did that work! That church broke all attendance records. We had to bring in chairs from classrooms. We set up about 20 home Bible studies, and there were 89 baptisms that year.

One day, while we were living in El Paso, I heard that Pepperdine University was going to offer a master's Degree in Religion in El Paso. I did not have a degree, and knew I was not eligible for a Masters, but when time came to sign up, I showed up. I explained that I had no degree, but I wanted to take the courses anyway. I asked if there was any way I could sit in on the classes. Could I audit? The representative said he would ask when he got back to Pepperdine. When he came back, he told me that the school would let me take the Master's Degree program, but I would only get undergraduate credit. I was delighted. That's what I did.

Pepperdine flew professors to El Paso on weekends. We had classes on Friday evenings and all day each Saturday. We had lots of homework. One semester was a reading semester, the next was a writing semester, and the third was a difficult passages semester. I made all A's. I was very glad I had taken that speed-reading course in Lubbock.

THE THREE STOOGES
COULD NOT HAVE DONE IT BETTER...

Tim finished his Spring semester at Lubbock Christian College and decided to come home to El Paso for the summer. My secretaries' daughter, Pam, also a student at LCC, had hitched a ride with him. His car broke down about 50 miles outside of El Paso. It was early morning, so Pam called her mother to pick them up. It was about 5:30am when Tim called me. He wanted me to pick him up at Pam's house and take him to pick up his car. He said it would have to be towed.

First, I called a wrecker service, but it was way too expensive. I told Jo I would go to a U-Haul place and rent a bumper hitch, which I did. I am not very good with mechanical things, but I thought Tim was. When I picked him up, I asked him if he knew how to remove the drive shaft from his car (I knew that much about towing a car). He said he did. We were all set. We had everything we needed. It shouldn't take long to remove the drive shaft from his car, hook up the tow bar to the cars, and be on our way, right? I had left the house at 6:00am.

The highway was not busy, so we made good time finding his car. I turned and pulled in front of his car, so I could back in position to attach the tow bar. It took Tim a while to get the drive shaft out, but he did, and he put it in the back of his station wagon. I attached the tow bar as best I could, and we hopped in my car and pulled onto the highway (there was hardly any traffic). I felt really good that it had not taken long, and we were on our way home. We had not gone far when I looked in the rear-view mirror and noticed Tim's car was coming loose from the tow bar. I told Tim and pulled over on the side of the road and stopped. I told Tim to sit tight, I would take care of it. I went back, and one of the nuts had come lose. I reattached it, made sure everything was secure and tightened, got back in the car, and away we went. I don't know how far we had gotten when I looked in the rear-view mirror and saw that Tim's car was loose again. When we stopped this time I told Tim, "I guess I didn't tighten the nuts tight enough." I tried again, and off we went. It happened a third time; his car came loose. This time, Tim got out with me. When we looked, we saw that we had lost one of the nuts. Tim said it must be on the highway. We took off the tow bar, put it in my car, locked up Tim's car, and went looking for the nut. He said I should drive slowly, and he would look for it. I thought that would be dangerous on the highway, but we would try. We drove very slowly along the highway for a very long time without seeing a single car. Suddenly, Tim said, "There it is! Stop!" I could see it sitting right in the middle of the highway. There were no cars in sight, so I stopped, and Tim got out and picked up the nut. We turned around and headed back to his car. We re-attached the tow bar which I had been tightening with my fingers, and this time, for some reason, I reached under the tow bar, and started turning a different nut that immediately showed me that if I tightened those nuts under the tow bar using a wrench, the tow bar would not come undone. I had finally figured out how to secure the tow bar. (I should have read the directions.) I asked Tim to bring me a wrench. He looked around for a time, and then said, "Oh, I left my tools back where we picked up my car. We have to go back and find them."

Once again, we secured his car by the side of the road, put the tow bar in my car, and headed back to see if we could find the place where his car had broken down, and find his tools which he kept in a woman's purse. Again, we drove slowly, but there was no traffic to speak of. I said I thought we had gone too far and missed the spot. Tim said to keep going. I could not believe we had gotten so far with all the trouble we had. Eventually, Tim yelled, "There. I see it." I turned around off the highway, and Tim jumped out of the car and got his bag of tools.

Finally. We now had it made. We had the tools. I now knew how to install the tow bar, so it would not come loose. We were on our way to get his car, attach it, and tow it home. I finally felt really good. Suddenly, I heard a strange noise. I said, "What's that noise, Tim? It sounds like a helicopter." I began looking out my windows for a helicopter. It sounded like one was right on top of us. Tim said, "I think we've got a flat." I realized he was right and pulled over and stopped. I thought, "What else can go wrong?"

It was the right rear tire. It was real flat. My car was a huge 9 passenger Ford Country Squire Station Wagon. I had a spare, and a jack. It was another setback, but it would not take too much time to get going again. I set the jack in place and started jacking up the car. When I thought it was high enough, I started taking off the wheel. I undid the nuts, and when I pulled the wheel off, I couldn't get it out from under the fender. I found that the car needed to be jacked up just a little more - just a notch or two. I went to the jack and pumped it once. The car rolled forward wedged itself on the jack and the tire. There was nothing we could do. We could not get the tire off, nor could we get the jack out from under the car. I had forgotten to put on the emergency brake. Now we were really stranded by the highway.

We looked both ways, and there wasn't a car in sight. I had forgotten my watch, and so had Tim. We had no idea what time it was but were sure it was way past noon. All we could do was stand there in the hot Texas sun and wait for a good-Samaritan to come along.

It seemed like hours had passed when a car zoomed by without even slowing down. A long time later, a car zoomed by from the other direction without slowing. I could not believe it. Surely someone would stop and help us. It was a long time later that a big semi-truck came along and stopped across the highway from us. He said he did not have the equipment to help us, but he had a CB and he would radio for help for us. We thanked him, and he went on his way.

It was at least a half hour later that two young Mexican men pulled to a stop across the highway from us. They were in an old pick-up truck they had restored. It was painted a bright shiny black. They sauntered across the highway (there was no traffic) and inspected our problem. They did not speak English. They decided they could help us. They sauntered back across the highway to their truck and brought back their jack. It, too, was painted a bright, shiny black. The jack part was very small. The base was about 8" square, and it stood about 6" tall. The arm that wound it up was about 10' long, and the handle to wind with was about 8". So, they slid that little thing in place under the axel and inserted that long winding-rod into the jack and started turning. The guy would turn 20 or 30 times, and the jack would go up about an inch. It was the silliest thing I ever saw. Just about then, two nice cars zoomed up, and stopped. Two young men got out, got their jacks, and in just a few minutes had us fixed and ready to go.

155

We went to El Paso without any more trouble. We took Tim's car to a shop and left it and took the tow bars back to U-Haul.

We got home about 6:00pm. I was really angry I had wasted a whole day. Jo wanted to know what happened to make us so late. What took us so long. I was furious and began telling her this story from the beginning. As I told her, she began to laugh. The more I told, the more she laughed. It made me more angry that she laughed at my troubles. She said I should listen to my story, it was funny. I began to see she was right. She thought it was a very funny story. I do too, now.

One day, while we were living in El Paso, Jo got suddenly sick. It was very strange. She just had no energy at all. She would get up, and walk from one chair to another, and sit down. I took her to our doctor neighbor next door (we went to his office), and he ran a lot of tests on her. Finally, he told us that as best as he could tell, she had "Addison's" disease. He told us that Addison's was incurable, and that she would have it the rest of her life. He said there were no doctors in El Paso that he thought were trained to help her in this unusual disease, and he recommended we find her a doctor in Dallas. At home, we told the kids, and talked about it a long time. I told Jo I didn't think I ought to be a preacher anymore, because she did not need to be a preacher's wife with Addison's. She asked what I would do? I said I would go back into the art business as a freelancer. She said I had not been in the art business for over 10 years, did I think I could get back in it? I told her that in 3 months I would be bringing home $1,000.00 a week or more or I wasn't trying.

John went with his mother, Jo, to Dallas, to find us a rent house. They did.

It was late summer of 1976. Tim had spent the summer with us and went back to LCC early to get ready for the Fall semester. I resigned from the church, borrowed $2,500.00,
156

and we packed two big U-Haul trucks full, Tom Barton drove one truck and John rode shotgun. I drove the other truck. Carol, who had taken Driver's Ed in the summer, but did not have a license, drove our car, and pulled a big trailer. Jo was a nervous wreck the whole way with Carol driving, but we were off to Dallas.

John and Tom were stopped by Highway Patrol and accused of drug trafficking. They wanted to look in the U-Haul truck, but I had the key, and was nowhere in sight. Sorry, no cell phones in those days. They had a hard time convincing the cops the truck was full of furniture only.

I had no visible means of support; I had borrowed $2,500.00, with no way of paying it back. My art portfolio was 10 years old, and I had not been a professional artist for 10 years, not since 1965, and it was now 1975. But there was not a doubt in my mind that I would find work, and in 3 months or less, I would be bringing home over $1,000.00 a week. I did.

Chapter 19

Maybe I ought to be
A Commercial Artist
When I grow up...

As we approached Dallas from El Paso, Jo and Carol had to lead the way because her mother was the only one who knew where the house was. They led us into Garland, a suburb in north Dallas.

They led us up to the front of a huge, beautiful, 2 story house Jo had rented. It had bay-windows on both sides of the lower front. It had 5 bedrooms and 3 bathrooms. It had a good-sized family room upstairs, four bedrooms and a bathroom. The fifth bedroom was downstairs with a large private bathroom. There was also a small powder room downstairs. To the right of the foyer was a formal living room and to the left was a formal dining room. Straight ahead was a very large kitchen with a big breakfast nook and beyond that a large den. It was in a very nice area of large two-story houses. Our front and back yards were filled with huge trees, and our back yard ended at a little stream. The rent in 1976 was just under $400.00. But, I had no visible means of support, and the rent would be due in 30 days. How did she rent it from Ebby Halliday, the largest realtor in Dallas, when I had no visible means of support, no job, no steady income? She never told me. Jo was amazing.

Not only did I have confidence that I would get work, but Jo did, too. We moved right in. (Remember, I had borrowed $2,500.00 in El Paso, to make this move. It was due in 90 days. I used some of it to rent the trucks, and for expenses to make the trip. We would use what was left of it as far as it would go, after we moved in.)

The very next day, I went looking for artwork. Bob Knight was a friend I had known since I had worked as a freelance artist in Dallas back in the early 1960s. I had called him about my coming back to Dallas, and he offered to let me office free in his studio until I got on my feet. He said he would feed me a little work along, but I could freelance all I wanted. He told me the "going rate" now was $25.00 an hour, not $10.00. So, the first thing I did that first day was to set up my cubicle. Bob had a big art studio, large enough to accommodate 10 or more artists. Currently, it was just Bob and one other artist. All the other cubicles were vacant. I could take my pick. Bob and I talked a while, and I learned that $25.00 an hour was just for paste-up and production work, but illustration and design went for $50.00 to $100.00 an hour. I found work that day. In just a few days, I had work orders for several thousand dollars. The jobs were all due in two or three weeks. I took the work orders to a local bank and borrowed a couple of thousand against the work orders. I would pay the bank off in 30 days. I opened an account at that bank. That bank Vice President and I worked together that way for a while, until I got my cash flow going. Banks can't do that anymore. No individual banker has that power anymore. Anyway, I was bringing home over $1,000.00 a week before we had been in Dallas 2 months. I had picked up IBM as a client, and they alone were feeding me more than $1,000.00 a month in work. I was making more in a week as an artist than I ever made in a month as a preacher.

We had not been in the Dallas area very long, in fact, it seemed like just a few days, and Jo started feeling much better. We took her to a doctor, and after giving her some tests, he told her, "I don't know what you had in El Paso, but it couldn't have been Addison's, because you don't have it now." He said, "In fact, you don't have anything now. You can go home and go on with your life."

Our house was just a couple of blocks from a large church of Christ, The Austin Street church of Christ. They had about 1000 members, maybe more. The first Sunday we were in Garland, we went there and placed our membership. That first Sunday we learned that it was their preacher's last Sunday. I got the impression that he had been fired though no one said so. I told the elders I would preach for them while they searched for a new preacher. Immediately, I was preaching for them every Sunday, taught Bible classes Sunday and Wednesday nights, yet worked for myself weekdays.

In about three months, the elders came to our house and offered me the job as their preacher. I turned down the job. It was the largest church ever to offer me a job. It was an affluent church, and probably would have paid me very well - much more than I had ever made before as a preacher, but I just had a bad feeling about their elders. I don't know what it was, but I just had a bad feeling.

Eventually, the church there hired a preacher, and I continued to lead singing some, and teach adult Bible classes often.

I flat "hit the jackpot" in Dallas as a freelancer. I attended the artist's luncheons again, and I went to the church of Christ preacher's luncheons every Friday at Wyatt's Cafeteria. The work I got from IBM was all illustration work. Remember that illustration work went for $100.00 per hour. I got tons of work (lots of it is still in my portfolio – ink drawings). We were really making lots of money.

I moved out of Bob Knight's studio and was invited to move into Graphic Illustrators Studio; Torg Thompson's studio. I got lots more work from Torg, and more elite clients that paid more. For Torg, I did work for the largest ad agencies in Dallas. Torg had painted a huge mural of the Day of Pentecost out at some cemetery for some very rich man who had died. It was privately housed with special lighting, a sound system and bleachers for over 100 people to view as Acts 2 was read by a professional speaker, recorded and played at certain times of the day. It was tragic that the burned down some years later destroying that marvelous mural and presentation.

John and Joe had a great Piano teacher when we lived in Lubbock, but we did not live there very long. And in El Paso, we could not find them a good teacher. They had a mediocre teacher, but we were not in El Paso long.

As soon as my art business began a fairly good cash-low, we began a search for a really good piano teacher for John and Joe. They both had the gift from God of extraordinary musical talent. Both of them did not learn music, they absorbed it like a sponge. We never once ever told either one of them to go practice your piano lessons. They almost fought each other over the piano to practice four hours a day and often into the night. We nearly had to drag one off to let the other one on. That piano was played constantly as long as either one of them was in the house. We had to find them the BEST piano teacher in Dallas. We did. We found **Mrs. Caroline Campbell.**

The only problem was, there were several problems. 1.) She taught in her home in South Oak Cliff, and we lived in Garland, 30 miles away. 2.) She had to see each boy twice each week; once for a piano lesson, and once for music theory. 3.) It was going to cost $200.00 each for them to take lessons from her. The boys started immediately. Of course, John could drive himself, but we needed another car. Jo took Joe and had to wait to take him home. $400.00 a month for piano lessons, not to mention music to buy, a car to buy, and gas. It was fall of 1975.

It was John's last year to be at home. He was in his Senior year in high school and was planning to attend ACU next Fall as a Piano Performance Major. He really took off with Mrs. Campbell and made great progress as a pianist. He

161

learned so much from her in music theory and music history that he "tested out" on those courses at ACU when he got there.

Chapter 20

When I grow up...
I want to be a preacher

I can't imagine why, but we moved to DeSoto, where I preached for the DeSoto church of Christ. I don't remember what happened to cause me to do that. I do know that I had lost the IBM account. They told me that they passed their work around to artists. It was their policy, and I had their account long enough, and now it was time for them to give their work to a different artist. It was most of my income. I was no longer sharing space with Bob Knight but had moved my office home and into the formal living room. The DeSoto church was going to help us buy a house in DeSoto. The church was 750 members (I think). I still had plenty of artwork to do and was still making more in art than the DeSoto church was going to pay me. Go figure.

As we were preparing to move from Garland to DeSoto in November of 1977, Carol did not want to change schools again in the middle of a semester. We discovered that, because of the advanced school system in Virginia, Carol had already accumulated enough credits to graduate high school, so she did. She was allowed to graduate Garland High School in November of 1977. She came back in the Spring of 1978 to go through the ceremonies with her classmates. We did not let Carol go to college at the young age of 17 but made her wait until the fall of 1978. After we moved to DeSoto, Carol found a job. We had also bought a lot of new and expensive furniture.

We move to DeSoto...

DeSoto, a suburb of Dallas, is way south. We were there from November of 1977 to August of 1978, but some significant things happened there in that short time.

First, Jo took over the Ladies' Bible Class. They had never had more than 25 or 30 to attend. Jo built the class to 85 almost immediately. She also started a "Mother's Day Out" program. (The concept came from our knowledge of the work of the great Madison Tennessee church where Ira North preached.) We offered to keep pre-school children at the church free of charge from 10am to 3pm on Tuesdays and Thursdays to give young mothers a day off. We, of course, would teach the children Bible stories. Our hope was to get the ladies to bring their children and husbands to church on Sundays. It was a very successful program. Many baptisms were the result of this good work.

Jo dearly loved the house we bought with the help of the church. When we sold the house and moved away, she didn't say a word. But she regretted selling and leaving that house the rest of her life. I think it was the one thing I did that hurt her deeply. She talked about it often. I have felt bad about not knowing how strongly she felt about the house at the time. I believe I would not have ever sold that house and moved from DeSoto.

Anyway, I could not seem to let go of some of my art clients, and soon an opportunity came along in art that was just too good to pass up. An Ad Agency offered to let me office in his space, and I would get to do all their art work on a freelance basis, plus my own clients. (An artist had had that position before for years and had been very successful.) I had been doing some freelance work for that agency, and they were very pleased. That is why I was invited. I resigned from the church and moved in with Sorenson/Evans Advertising (one man and his female assistant). We continued to live in our house until we could get it sold. It was more than 30 miles one way from our house in DeSoto to my office in the

Carillon Towers in North Dallas. All my clients were in North Dallas. We were going to have to move to North Dallas.

The fifty-dollar car wash...

Tex gave me an old Nash Ambassador car that I could use as a trade-in to buy a new car. I wanted to buy a second car to use as a business car. The Ambassador ran; it was huge, and it was dirty. I decided to wash it before I tried to trade it in. I had recently heard on TV that I could get more money on a trade-in if it was clean, and especially if the motor was clean.

I drove it to a do-it-yourself car wash place and washed the car. Then, I opened the hood and washed the motor. When I got in the car to drive home, it would not start. I realized I had gotten the distributor wet. I had nothing to dry it with, but it was an extremely hot day in Dallas. I think it was 114, so I decided to push the car out onto the parking lot into the sun. I could then open the hood, and the noonday sun would dry the distributor in a New York minute. I began to push the big car, but I was not big enough or strong enough to do more than rock it back and forth a little. A big fellow came to help me, and we got it out of the washing stall and onto the parking lot. I had not realized before, that the parking lot was not level, but slanted rather steeply. Once on the parking lot, it began to roll downhill. I started running alongside to try opening the door and jump in to put on the brakes and put it in Park. It was rolling too fast, and I ran along until I realized I wasn't going to catch it. At the end of the parking lot, was a curb, and a fence to a neighbor's yard. The car jumped the curb, knocked down the fence, and stopped at an apple tree. I had to call a tow truck to get the car out and take it and me home. Later, I got a good trade-in price, and bought a neat little car. It cost me $50.00 to tow my car home. I call this story **MY $50.00 CAR WASH.**

From six children to nine...

165

Shortly after we put our house up for sale in DeSoto, we got a strange phone call. A woman called saying she was interested in buying our house because she was looking for a larger house than she had. The reason was that she suddenly had twin baby girls to take care of. They belonged to her daughter. Her daughter could not take care of them. Jo was talking to her, and I don't know all that was said, but they talked for a good long time. When she hung up, Jo said the woman was bringing the baby girls for us to keep while the grandmother ran some errands.

It wasn't long until she came and brought two of the cutest twin baby girls. They were just a few months old. The grandmother then explained more of their family problems and asked us to keep them for a couple of weeks. Jo, of course, agreed. After the woman left, Jo saw that she left no diapers, no clothes, no food, nothing. We had to go out immediately and buy all kinds of things to be able to keep these babies.

The babies' father was a drug addict and was in jail. Their mother was a topless dancer in a nightclub and was living with a black man. The mother was 18. Nobody ever showed up, and no phone numbers were working numbers. We had twin baby girls, Sonya and Tonya. We took them with us when we moved to Richardson. Eventually, we sold our house and moved to Richardson.

Chapter 21

I think, when I grow up... I want to be a Commercial Artist

We move from DeSoto to Deep Valley in Richardson...
It was August of 1978. We rented a nice, big 2 story house on Deep Valley Dr., just one block from the campus of the University of Texas at Dallas. After I quit preaching, I moved my art business into Sorenson/Evans Advertising in the Carillon Towers, and my business began to take off again.

Jo was in hog-heaven with those twin babies. And their older brother came with them. Andy was two. The cutest little tow-headed boy you could ever want. She got to see the twins when they first sat up, when they first began to crawl, when they spoke their first word, and when they took their first step. We bought furniture for them, and whatever they needed. Their mother came to see them one time. She looked at them like she did not know what they were. She had no idea which twin it was (but we did), nor did she try to pick them up. She was strange. The father got out of jail and came to see them. He wanted to know all about them. He was much older than the mother. He must have been in his late 40s. He wanted us to have them and wanted us to go to court to get them. He said he would take our side and did not think their mother would care. He said the girls and Andy would have a better chance in life with us than with him or their mother.

We got custody of the girls and Andy. Realizing that when the girls reached their teens, we would be in our 60s, we decided to contact a church of Christ adoption agency and find them a younger family, which we did.

I did very well in Richardson. We attended the Waterview congregation, and after a time, I was made a deacon.

We lived several years on Deep Valley Drive in Richardson, a suburb of Dallas, after the three little ones were adopted.

One of the things we did soon after moving to Deep Valley was to buy a 5'10" KAWAI grand piano (not a Baby Grand) for John and Joe. Their teacher, Carolyn Campbell, insisted the boys had to play and practice on a good grand piano. So I sent Jo and the boys down to Munsell's Piano & Organ store to buy a grand piano. Munsell's Piano warehouse had nothing but grand pianos. It was huge, and there were so many pianos to choose from. I don't know how long they looked, but each boy tested and tried every piano in the warehouse, some of them several times before coming to a decision. They each chose the same piano for the same reasons. No disagreements at all. What are the chances of that happening? The piano cost $8,000.00.

Have I ever mentioned that I love music?

When we first moved to Dallas in the early 1950's, I was delighted to find the radio station there – WRR. They played classical music round the clock.

I quit listening to popular music in the early 1950s. I liked the "big band" music of the 1940's, but I especially liked the singers of that era - Sinatra, Bing Crosby, Nat King Cole, Doris Day, etc. I could not abide Elvis Presley, the Beatles, and all the rest of that bunch that followed until today (Rock music), so I quit listening, and switched to the classical stations. I decided rock music was responsible for the "hippie" movement, and the drug abuse that invaded our country. They were, in the beginning, "the great unwashed."

As long as, and whenever we lived in Big D, I listened to WRR radio. When we lived in the Washington, DC area, I always listened to WGMS (Washington's Great Music Station).

I was not raised in the country. I was never a country boy, so I have never liked country/western music.

I heard on the Dallas station, a recording of the Dallas Symphony Orchestra, and they announced the opening of their Fall season in just a few weeks. We Had just moved to Deep Valley Drive in Richardson, so, one day I came home with two season tickets to the Dallas Symphony for Jo and me. They were cheap seats - $5.00 each in the 3rd balcony, but for every Friday night from September through February. Needless to say there were some Friday nights we just could not make it, but we made most of them.

We really enjoyed going to the symphony. One Friday night, there was a performance of the Dallas Symphony Orchestra with the Dallas Symphony Chorus. I turned to Jo and said, "I would really like to be a part of that." I had not sung with a chorus since high school, but I felt like I really wanted to try to sing with the Dallas Symphony Chorus. I had no idea how to go about it. I did not know where to go or who to see about singing with them. I sort of forgot about it.

All my life I had loved classical music. Before I married, I had lots of classical records that I played often. After we married I played lots of my classical music often, hoping my children would grow up appreciating great music. It was played in my car and in my house. It was a big part of my whole life. My high school chorus was exceptionally good. We sang most all the Messiah, and we had to memorize it. We were not allowed to have our music. I was good enough a sight reader and singer in high school to be a section leader. One could walk into our house any day from the time Jo and I married till this day, and you might hear an opera, or some other classical music.

169

In the Spring of 1979, I was listening to WRR, Dallas' classical music station, and I heard that the Dallas Symphony Chorus was holding auditions for new members at the University of Texas at Dallas (and they gave the time and date and place). It was a block from my house. They had said I should sing two art songs. I went home, dug out a couple of pieces of sheet music - one I remember was Comfort Ye from the Messiah, but I don't remember the other. When the time came, I went to audition. There were several people there to hear me. I have to admit I was a little nervous, but once I started singing, I was fine. When I was done, they said I was in. I could hardly believe it. I was overjoyed. I gave my name and address and phone number and said I would sing 2nd tenor. **I was 48 years old.**

The chorus was beginning its 2nd year when I got in. They were having some problems with the choral director they had started with, so they fired him. The first year I was in, they had an interim director. The next year, they got a really good director that stayed with them. He made it harder to get in by requiring two art songs - one in a foreign language, a sight-reading test, and a music theory test. I managed to get in for 10 straight years.

I really loved to sing in the Dallas Symphony Chorus. I moved from tenor to bass soon after I started. There were 226 in the Chorus by the time I left. It was glorious in sound. When we performed, I stood behind the Percussion section, but I could see the String section, as well as others. What a joy to watch a great orchestra perform from close up and sing with them under the direction of world class music Conductors and sing the world's greatest music. We had some of the world's greatest guest conductors.

Then, I think it was at the start of my third year that our choral conductor (I still can't remember his name) announced that the Dallas Opera was needing more singers in their chorus, and if any of us were interested in singing with them we should audition at such-and-such a place at such-and-such a time (I don't remember), but I did. An old man that looked like he was 100, and spoke only Italian, asked us, one at a time, to stand up on a little stagehand our music to a pianist, and sing our aria. I sang only a couple of lines, and he stopped me and said I was in. The Dallas Opera paid singers Union wages, so I had to join the Musician's Union (I don't remember what I was paid).

They also required that we all have a voice teacher. I asked a group of opera singers if they could recommend a voice teacher, and I got two names they said were the top two teachers in Dallas. Madelyn Sanders was one, and the other was Marilyn Walker. I auditioned for each of them and was rejected by Mrs. Sanders (I would have rejected her as well) and accepted by Marilyn Walker. Marilyn was the best I had had since my first teacher that was so good in Austin, when I was 16. Marilyn was just younger than I was and was a great teacher. She had students that had made it into several of the nation's best opera companies. She even had students that now sang in the New York Metropolitan Opera. I really made good progress with her. Marilyn helped me memorize my music for the Dallas Opera. It was hard. We, of course, had to memorize all our music in a foreign language. We had to act in the opera, and, in opera, nobody has a microphone. Rehearsals were 5 nights a week from 7 - 10. We gave 3 performances; Friday night, Saturday afternoon, and Saturday night. I don't remember how we worked it out with the Dallas Symphony Chorus, but Chorus performances were later in the year, or something. I managed to do both, but it was really hard to do and keep up with my art business which was doing very well. In those days, the Dallas Opera did 4 operas a year. I had always dreamed of singing in an opera. Of course, my dream was to be the leading man in the Met, but I was on stage and singing with stars of the Met that came to Dallas and sang leading roles. I stood next to them, and back stage, heard them warming up - huge, magnificent voices. I, as did we all, had a "dresser" to help me in and out of costume (all "dressers" were homosexuals). I got to meet all the "imported" singers. It was a great experience for me.

I was in both choruses the next year, but the third year I decided I just could not handle both, so I dropped out of the Opera chorus. It was just too demanding. I continued taking voice lessons from Marilyn Walker, however, the rest of the time we lived in Dallas.

I look back now at 21 years in Symphony choruses, and two in the Dallas Opera, and I think of all the many pieces of great music by the world's greatest composers that I was privileged to sing with great musicians, great singers, and great conductors, and I feel so blessed and so thankful that I was allowed to do that. I loved it all so much.

The first night I went to chorus practice with the Dallas Symphony, they passed out our music, and we went through each piece, singing from 7 to 10 pm with 15 minutes break. I was overwhelmed. I had not looked at music that hard to read since high school, and this was much harder. When I went home, I was discouraged. The next Monday night, I told Jo I was just going to chorus to turn in my music. It was just too hard for me. She said it was not too hard for me, that I just needed to stay with it and try to learn it. She said she knew I could do it if I just worked at it. And she practically pushed me out the door. She had to encourage me a good bit at first to keep me from dropping out. Sure enough, eventually I began to read the music and learn what I was doing. I would never have made it without Jo's encouragement.

I like to read, too...

I didn't use to. I hated reading when I was young, except for reading the Bible. I read the Bible often but was not a "daily Bible reader" until I was 19 or 20.

172

I never really read a novel cover to cover all the way through high school. I bluffed my way somehow. They had comics about famous novels back then, and I read those, or I would read the first 4 or 5 chapters, 3 or 4 through the middle, and the last 5. I could make a convincing bluff, and pass a test, barely.

When I was grown, married, and had several kids, I saw Robert Ludlum in a TV ad. He was said to be the foremost Spy novelist in the world. My interest was pricked, and I bought, THE BOURNE IDENTITY. I not only could not put it down, I could not sit down to read it. I would start out sitting down to read, but would get so excited, I would have to stand up and walk around. When I finished that one, I got his next, then his next, etc. From then on, I was an avid reader of novels. I read one after another. I carried them with me and read everywhere I had a moment to pause; even at traffic lights. In my art business, I had clients all over Dallas. I was often in my car driving. In all those years, I was only honked at twice. I had great peripheral vision. At one point, I was reading 40 to 50 novels a year. I am still an avid reader.

After I took that speed reading course at LCU, I really read a lot of books for a while. I have already discussed my Bible reading habits. Name any book of the Bible and I have read it well over 160 times. I ought to know something about it. I have also read a lot of different English translations – more than 25, I think. I still have most of them, and they are pretty well marked up with underlines and my marginal notes and comments from Genesis through Revelation. It was some years before I ever thought about how many times I had read the Bible through. I had never numbered my readings. I began numbering them, I don't remember when, but you can see on the blank fly leaf of most of them where I began marking:

Began reading:

1.) 3-15-78; finished, 8-23-78.

2.) 8-24-78; finished, 1-19-79, etc.

I have a New King James Version that shows it was read 10 times, and the dates. I recently finished a 6th reading of a New American Standard Version. There are not many English Versions I have not read, and many of them several times. At one point in my life, I probably owned 25 or maybe 30 Bibles.

It's a matter of "What if?" –

What if there is no God? – Atheism is a matter of "What if there is no God?" It is the explanation of "in the beginning" if the God of the Bible does not exist.

What if the God of the Bible does exist? The Bible is the alternative explanation of "in the beginning." Which do you believe and why? I believe the Bible account, and the more I read the Bible, the more convinced I am that it is true. It attests to itself, and it is reasonable.

As an artist, one time I was asked by a client to produce a document that would appear to be 200 years old. I was able to do that to my client's satisfaction. The document was not one year old, but it appeared to be 200 years old. It was used only as an advertisement, not for any other use. Recently, on TV, an artist, painter, was interviewed who had deceived the world's greatest art experts into believing his paintings were done by other artists, dead hundreds of years ago, and his copies of old masters' paintings appeared to be hundreds of years old. Many of his paintings are still fooling the experts. If such fallible people can fool the world's greatest experts, surely a God such as is described in the Bible as all powerful, has the power and ability to create a world that looks billions of years old. Think about this. God created Adam from dust, formed a man, breathed into him the breath of life, and Adam became a living man. How old did Adam appear to be the instant he came to life? Thirty? But he was not 30 years old. If God could create a man that appeared to be 30 the instant he came to life, why could that God not create a world in a day that appeared to be billions of years old? How can you place limits on an all-powerful God?

Over and over and over through the Bible God says He created the universe in six days and rested on the seventh day. When you study evolution, and compare it to the Bible, it seems to me the weight of evidence is on the side of the Bible.

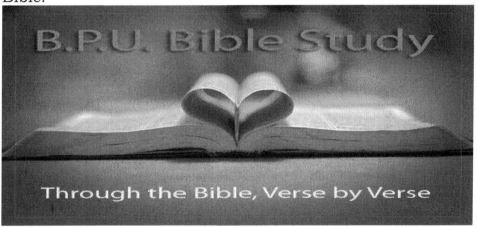

B.P.U. Bible Study

Through the Bible, Verse by Verse

Atheistic or Theistic evolutionists both deny the truth of the Bible. Evolution limits the power of God, rejects the Bible account of creation, and degrades mankind. I want to make clear my views on evolution because that gives a sense of how I think and what I am like. What I think is that to rejection of Biblical authority, denies the truth about Jesus, the fall of mankind, the very idea of sin, and opposes all Biblical ethics. The "theory" of evolution is so far-fetched and absurd I cannot understand why anyone would accept such unmitigated nonsense in exchange for the sublime words of Geneses 1:1: "In the beginning, God..." I think those words are pretty clear. It is, of course my opinion, but it is based on many years of study of both evolution and the

Bible. A large majority of evolutionists have not studied the Bible much if at all.

I stayed with Sorenson/Evans Advertising some years, I don't recall how many, but not many. Sorenson/Evans Advertising consisted of two persons; Bob Sorenson (of an indeterminable age}, and his Personal Assistant (a young woman who served as Greeter, Secretary, Bookkeeper, Proofreader, and whatever else an Advertising Agency needs). I, remember, was a freelance artist who worked in the closet. Actually, it was little more, it was a supply room. I occupied about 6' X 10', but I did have a nice window on my right. We were on the 7th floor of the Carillon Twin Towers, about a block or so from the LBJ Freeway. Really nice building, location, and offices.

Evans, of the Sorenson/Evans duo, I never saw, and eventually, I think, was dropped from the name of the Agency.

Bob Sorenson and his Assistant, with a little help from me, took in between 1 and 2 million a year. You can see why that big Agency in Abilene, with 40 employees, folded so quickly. I had already called on several ad agencies in Dallas that made over a million or two a year that had only a very few employees before I moved to Abilene. When I heard they had 40 employees, I thought they must have a thousand clients. When I found out how few clients they had, I figured they were doomed to fail. That was another reason I started looking to go back to Dallas so soon.

Bob Sorenson had some really good clients, and I did some of my best work as a commercial artist working for him and picked up some of my best clients. I even won an award working for Bob Sorenson. I designed a double-page ad for an electronics magazine, and won a plaque for The Most Readable Ad. The plaque is in my debris somewhere.

176

I also designed and produced one-page, front & back, full color, slick page "Data Sheets" by the hundreds for $1,000.00 each or more. I did many, full color, slick page brochures at $500.00 per page, many as large as 16 to 18 pages. I did Annual Reports that went for $1,000.00 per page, and most of them were 16 to 20 pages. Those were my charges to Sorenson, who knows what Sorensen charged his clients. I really made a lot of money in those years. We had three or four cars then.

I was so busy during those years, working so hard, singing in the Dallas Symphony Chorus (I designed their LOGO, had it put on blue "Golf" shirts and blue sweaters imprinted in white, that virtually all 226 Chorus members bought. I had the design printed on the Chorus' Stationary and Business cards, etc., I sang in the Dallas Opera, did other freelance work I will tell you about later, preached on occasion, and often taught Bible classes, that I neglected to keep up with my kids as I should have and for that, I am very sorry.

When we moved to Dallas from El Paso in 1975, Tim went back to Lubbock, to LCC because Sue lived in Lubbock. It was not long until Tim dropped out of LCC, and he and Sue married in June of 1977. Of course, we went to their wedding, I performed their ceremony. They had a son born January 2, 1983, Nicholas. There was a big snowstorm that day.

John was graduated from high school in the spring of 1977 and started Abilene Christian University as a Piano Performance Major in the fall of 1978. He came within 15 hours of finishing when he dropped out, came home and married Tina. I performed their wedding. Their precious little daughter, Natalie was born in October of 1983, but the marriage didn't last. Tina cheated on John, and they divorced. Tina got Natalie.

Carol graduated high school in November of 1978 and went to Abilene Christian University in the fall of 1979. She got

177

sick, and dropped out at mid-term, and went to Lubbock Christian in the fall of '79, where she met and married Ron Guzman on January 1, 1980. I performed their wedding also.

I don't know how long I worked with Bob Sorenson in his agency, but it wasn't many years. He was not easy to get along with.

A lot of things seem to all run together at times. If Jo was still alive, she would recall every detail, but I don't pay that close attention.

1983 comes along somewhere in these years. Nicholas was born on January 2 of that year. (I tend to get things out of chronological order. Nicholas was born before Natalie.)

I had a good many other clients than just Sorenson. His ego was bigger than mine, if you can believe that, and the clash of egos was part of our problem. He resented my working on my client's projects while I was in his office and putting them ahead of his projects even though I had to prioritize in order of due dates.

I also had some very good outside clients. I was getting work from the largest ad agency in Dallas, Bozell & Jacobs (far larger than that little 40 employee agency in Abilene). B&J had Pepsi, and I did lots of their work, but I had to go downtown to their offices. I don't know how many floors they occupied in the high rise building they were in. I did work for other agencies as well. I also did work for a large commercial art studio, Gaither & Davy. They had about 40 artists working for them, but they did a lot of work for Texas Instruments, and needed an artist that was especially good at Technical Illustration (I have one good example in my portfolio). Ironic, isn't it, that I never made $3.00 an hour working for T.I., but Gaither & Davy paid me $50.00 an hour to do T.I. work. No telling what they charged T.I. for my work.

Then I had several direct clients – direct with a business. I would sometimes act as their ad agency myself, brokering their printing, placing magazine insertion orders, etc. I would get ad agency rates for those services as well as for my art.

To be a freelance commercial artist, you must be able to do just about any kind of art a client might need. You had to be versatile. You had to be very good at design. You might be asked to design a new logo for a new company that was starting up. You might be asked to design a series of brochures for a company introducing a new series of products. You may be asked to design a trade show booth for a company, and so on. You may be given some rough drawings to produce nice drawings from. There is no telling what a potential client will ask of you.

On any given morning, I would go into my studio and look at all the different jobs I had to do. Often there were as many as 30 to 50 different jobs I had to do (not all due that day, of course). I have had as many as 100. I would list all my jobs to do that day in order of priority, which one was first, second, etc. A man once told me how Indians trained young boys to become braves. They would dig a pit, fill it with snakes, give a young Indian boy a club, and give him one instruction; "Kill the one that's nearest." That's what it's like to be a freelance commercial artist. In all my years, I never missed a deadline. I have worked all night, but never missed a deadline.

One of my best such clients was Essex Windmills. Yep, those windmills you see on farms and ranches when you are driving out in the country. Essex was the world's largest maker and distributor of windmills. I did him a new Corporate Identity Program: I designed a new logo for the company that was to be used on everything – all stationary, envelopes, business cards, and all other business papers like invoices contracts, and the like. It was to be used on all windmills, all signage, corporate vehicles, etc. I designed brochures, ads, instruction manuals, and more stuff than you can think of and I can remember. What a wonderful client – he always paid "johnnie on the spot," on delivery (he would make me sit down, while he wrote me a check for the full amount). No check ever bounced.

Eventually, I moved my studio home again, but clients did not respond well to that, so it was not very long until a friend and I rented space in a building about a block from Sorenson's. Our rent was $1,000.00 a month. We paid $500.00 each. The building was really nice, and they put in nice new red carpet, rich-grey metal walls, and we moved in. It was great.

As it turned out, there was an ad agency on the same 7th floor we were on. When they learned I was on their floor (so handy), they asked to see my portfolio, were impressed, and began feeding me work. It was a very big agency (about 30 or so employees).

I simply could not handle all the work, so we set Jo up with an art table and all the trimmings. She actually handled all the work that came from our neighbor, and then some.

About that time, John was trying to get started as an insurance agent, so we started babysitting our precious little granddaughter, Natalie, in our office. She loved to look out our great big windows down at the traffic on the Dallas North Tollway. We had a grand time. Natalie was born October 15, 1983. John met and married Pam Harmon in 1995.

It was a great marriage, made to last. Pam is an Interior Designer, like my cousin, Bob Henry.

Also, about that time I got a new client, and was asked to illustrate a series of Bible school material. It was for Gospel Teachers Publishers. That was a project that was going to take a couple of years or more. It was graded material from toddlers through high school. After some starts and stops, we determined that Jo had the better grasp of the project, and a better technique of illustrating the Bible stories than I did, so she took over that job completely, illustrating every story in the Bible from Adam and Eve in the Old Testament through the final scenes of the New Testament book of Revelation. She illustrated every story in full color, making color separations for the printer). All her original art for that project is in our storage, including the full-color separations.

We loved living on Deep Valley Drive in Richardson. Ii was a street that turned off a through street and circled around back into the same through street. There was a Junior High School on the through street at the first turn on to Deep Valley, and it had a full-size track behind the school. Richardson is a "high class" suburb of Dallas, so the school was very nice as was the neighborhood. Jo and I often walked around our block after dinner. It was a fairly large block. In the summers, we walked around the track. It was good that it was about a half a block from our house, because Jim and Joe finished Junior High there.

We lived on Deep Valley long enough for Jim and Joe to finish High School at J. J. Pearce in Richardson. Jim made the Gymnastics team and was especially proficient on the Pommel Horse and the Rings. He almost went to State on the Pommel Horse and would have if he had not gotten a severe problem with his Thyroid gland. He lost a lot of weight suddenly and got very weak. He did, however, set a school record on the Pommel Horse. I don't know if it still stands.

Joe did very well in A Cappella chorus. I designed (for free) the School logos for the School Choirs (still in use) and Gymnastic team (still in use).

We lived 7 years on Deep Valley Drive, and one day, we got a call from our rental agent that the owners were being transferred back home from Saudi, Arabia, and wanted their house back. We had to move whether we wanted to or not.

We move to Plano... 1985...

We found a very nice tract house in Plano that was all on the ground floor. It was large, had 4 bedrooms (3 were somewhat small, but it was just right for us since our family was down to just Jo and me and Jim and Joe.

One day, Joe brought home a little dog, and I mean little. He fit in my hand with room to spare. Ugliest little dog I ever saw. It could easily win any Ugliest Dog contest anywhere. We called him Fudge, because he looked like he had Fudge candy smeared across his lips. He was also snaggle-toothed. Jo taught him to stay on a small bath matt just inside the back door. That dog would go outside into our fenced back yard to run, do his business, and then come in and lie down on his little pad. He had food and water by him, but that dog did not go from his mat to anywhere else in the house ever in his life. Amazing.

For a short time, Tim and Sue and Nicholas moved from Lubbock to Plano. One day they were visiting with us, and Sue suggested Jo and I take a vacation (The only vacations we ever took were when I was a preacher, and then we only went to visit our parents, and, of course, that one time we to Cape May, New Jersey with the Magreer family when I preached at Springfield, Virginia). Sue suggested we ought to at least take a day and go to "Wet and Wild." I said, "Yeah. She'll get wet, and I'll get wild." That really cracked Sue up. We never took that vacation.

I loved to read, and one day I was home, reading some exciting spy novel, and John came by for a visit. I told John I would like to write a novel someday, but I could not think of a plot. John said, "I have a plot for you, dad." I said, "You do?" John said, "What if somebody tried to blow up the Dome of the Rock." I nearly jumped out of my skin. It was a perfect plot. I knew exactly how I needed to approach it, and I had a storyline already in mind.

I got myself a big 3-ring notebook, lots of lined paper, and started writing in ink, in longhand (I didn't know shorthand). Computers were just now coming into prominence, but I was an unbeliever. I needed to get some kind of writing machine, but in 1987, I could not decide what to get, so I wrote in longhand, in a notebook. It took me five years to write the novel, but eventually I got a computer and rewrote it four or five times. More about my novel later.

My father died December 23, 1987. He was 80 years old. He always said he would only live to be 80. He said that was all we were promised by God, and he would quote Psalm 90:10, *"The days of our years are threescore years and ten; and if by reason of strength they be fourscore years yet is their strength labor and sorrow; for it is soon cut off, and we fly away."* I thought it remarkable that he called his own years. Dad got sick and died in just a couple of months. He had prostate cancer.

It all begins to fall apart...

For several years, I had heard that computers were going to be used in commercial art. It was inconceivable to me that a machine could be used to do commercial art. Like I said, I was an unbeliever. Jo, however was a believer, and warned me of their coming, and urged me to buy a Mackintosh. I kept putting it off, telling her I just did not believe computers would be a threat to my business.

It must have been 1986 that the ad agency on my floor merged with another agency and took over the entire 7th floor except for my office. They came to see me one day, and offered to take over all my clients, but let me still service them as an account executive, do all their art work, and make the same income from them as I was making, but I would let their agency have my space, so they could have the whole floor. Jo and I would work for their agency, and also do artwork for them as well. They had a contract that spelled it all out. It looked like a good deal, especially since my roommate had just taken chapter 7 bankruptcy and had moved out leaving me with the full $1,000.00 a month rent. They actually saved my life. The "Oil Crunch" had hit about that same time, and while I had no oil accounts, all businesses cut back on their advertising severely.

It seems only a few days later, an IRS agent called on me to announce that they were not happy with my last year's return. They wanted to audit my return.

After we moved into the agency, I noticed computers everywhere, even a few in the art department. I still said, when you sit down at a computer, you are limited to what is built into the computer, but when I sit down at a drawing board I am not limited by anything but my imagination and talent and skill as an artist.

The IRS agent came back some weeks later, and said they were so unhappy with what they found in my last year's return that they have decided to look at 5 years back and wanted all my records.

In the meantime, the agency really fell in love with Jo. She turned out to be the best "paste-up" artist they had ever seen. She was better and faster than anyone they had ever seen.
The problem was, we were not making the money we could make freelancing. We had an "out clause" in our contract, so I opted out. It made them FURIOUS. I think it was Jo they did not want to lose.

We moved our studio home again, but the "Oil Crunch" was killing us. Some months our income dropped to $800.00. We were going under. I was desperate.

The IRS came back and said we owed $5,000.00 in back taxes. If my business was like it had been when we first moved to Richardson, I could have easily made a payout deal, but not now. I had not lost any clients, they were just not doing any advertising to speak of right now.

I went to see the big art studio I had done work for, Gaither and Davy, and their studio consisted of the two of them, one air-brush artist (who was a freelancer just sharing an office with them), a secretary/bookkeeper, and a Photostat operator. They let me have freelance space, and fed me work along, and with their work and my clients, we limped along, but cut way down on our living expenses. We gave up all but two cars.

I found me an IRS lawyer who said he could get me out of my IRS problems, and not to worry. He was a former IRS agent, and said he was certain he could take care of my problem. After a few weeks, he came to see me, and told me he had convinced them that I was just stupid and did not know how to fill out my own forms. He said that was the only way to keep me out of prison. Then a few weeks later, I was back in trouble with the IRS. I called my lawyer only to find out he had run away with his secretary to leave his wife. I found a CPA who said he could take care of me.

Working with Gaither and Davy did not work out, and I got caught in a situation I had no control over. I had some clients that went chapter 7 bankruptcy, owing me a total of $25,000.00. I was forced into chapter 7 bankruptcy myself. If I had been a better businessman, I would have incorporated my art business. I operated under the name, "T Square Studio," but I never incorporated under that named. It would have saved my name and my money.

Dick Norman *specialist in creativity*

DICK NORMAN ADVERTISING ART/DESIGN

That was it. I shut down my art studio, and we lost
everything, the grand piano, cars, credit cards, everything.
My CPA took over my finances and gave me an allowance to
live on each month. I told Jo the only other thing I could do
was preach. So, I searched for churches seeking a preacher
in our brotherhood periodicals. I found a church in Corpus
Christi, contacted them, and made arrangements to meet
with them, preach for them and interview with them. I did,
was hired, and Jo and I moved to Corpus Christi.

Chapter 22

FOUR TERRIBLE YEARS

It was 1989 when we moved to Corpus. Jim and Joe stayed in Dallas. Corpus is the best kept secret in Texas. It is a beautiful city.

The church was once the largest in the city, but it was dying. The suburban churches were growing. I did not last 3 months until I resigned. We were facing serious problems.

Jo went back to Dallas and moved in an apartment with Jim and Joe. She worked 3 jobs while getting her GED. Then, she continued on to get an Associate Degree from a Junior college. She made the highest grades on her GED, and 4.0 on her Associate's studies. It was the hardest four years of her life.

I stayed a while in Corpus. I found a man who had an ad agency that I had worked for in Dallas. In fact, I had been his art director. He needed an art director but would only pay me $1,000.00 a month but said I could freelance as well. That was not near enough. I could not find anything else, so I went to Chicago to try to find artwork. I was able to find some art work.

Working in Chicago was interesting. I called on an agency in Naperville, a suburb of Chicago. They had two artists that worked exclusively on computers, but neither of them were illustrators, so they were glad to see me. They wanted me to draw a pen and ink cartoon image of a client to be used in a number of ways and sizes, and many other illustrations. Like I said, computers are limited, I'm not. I made $50.00 an hour working for them, but that was not enough in Chicago's economy.

Another agency I worked with for a time had a young blond girl as Art Director. She had no computer, but her Assistant Art Director did. Still, they had work for me. I did a lot of "paste-up and production" work as well as some illustration work. All work I did for them, I did on their premises. They paid me $25.00 an hour for paste-up, and $50.00 an hour for illustration.

One day, the blond Art Director had a large piece of heavy duty tracing paper on her drawing board, and she was discussing something with her assistant. They were whispering. I was pasting up a job but was curious about what they were discussing. In a moment, The Art Director said aloud, "But this is the design they chose, and I can't figure out how to do the finished art." Her assistant said, "Don't ask me." Then the Art Director picked it up and held it so I could see it. It was a pencil sketch of a double-page spread, full-color ad for a client that was to run in a major trade publication. At first glance, I could see that the Art Director had "designed herself into a corner." To do the finished art would be difficult, but not impossible. I said to her, "I know three ways the finished art can be done. The young girls had forgotten I was in the building. They turned to look at me like I was crazy. I got up and explained the three ways of production art to get the art ready for the printer at the magazine. Then, I told them the easiest and cheapest way. I ended up doing the job because neither of them possessed the artistic skill to do the job. I was 63 years old and had lots of experience. They paid me $50.00 an hour to do that job.

In that same ad agency, the Art Director brought me a couple of IV "thingies." You know, those things they put in your veins in the hospital. She said she had designed a series of wall posters for doctor's offices, for a bunch of different configurations of IVs. She wanted me to estimate what I would charge to draw the different configurations of IVs.

After studying them a few moments, I told her that the agency was paying me $25.00 an hour, and that I would do them for that. She told her bosses and came back to me and said they did not want an hourly rate, but a by-the-piece rate. I studied the IVs again. You have seen IVs; thin little tubes, bags, clips, etc., all very complicated, and drawn in ink. I gave her a price of $250.00 each. She came back and said my price was too high. They would look for another illustrator. I wanted the job really badly, so I said, "What about half that? What about $125.00 each?" They agreed to $125.00 each. I got $5,000.00, but it turned out, I did the drawings in pencil (they loved the pencil drawings) much faster than I ever dreamed I could do them. If they had paid me $25.00 an hour, the job would have only cost them $1,000.

Joe joined the Navy, and graduated Boot Camp while I was in Chicago. Jo came up for his graduation. Jo went back to Dallas, and I went to New Orleans.

Jo's brother, Charles, developed cancer, and was given about a year to live. Jo wanted to be with him that last year, so Charles got her a job at Scott & White Hospital in Temple and let her live in a two-bedroom house trailer behind his house in Heidenheimer, a little suburb of Temple, Texas.

There was nothing for me in New Orleans, so I joined Jo in Heidenheimer in 1992. The little suburb had no stoplights but did have a flashing yellow light. There was also one of the busiest train tracks in Texas that passes by our two-bedroom trailer house about 100 yards away. It sounded like it went through the bedroom at the other end of our trailer house. I had taken my Social Security the previous year at 62, so we were paying Charles rent on the trailer house. He helped us get a little used Ford Festiva. It was so small we didn't get in it, but put it on.

Now, with my Social Security and Jo's hospital income, we decided we could afford to move into Temple. We found the cutest little two-story row-houses and were able to rent one.

We enjoyed our nice place, and Temple. We loved the little church in Heidenheimer, and they welcomed me, letting me lead singing some, and even preach some. I worked a while at Dillard's, then at Montgomery Ward, till they went out of business. I found a little freelance art to do. I got $25.00 an hour, but not much work.

Jo hated her job, it was so hard and stressful. So, in 1993, she went on Social Security, and in 1994, I decided to go back into preaching if I could find a church that would hire a 65-year-old preacher. I did, would you believe.

Jo's brother died of cancer the year we moved to Florida.

Chapter 23
When I grow up...I want to be a Preacher

A little church in Punta Gorda, Florida invited me to fly down, preach for them and interview for the position of preacher. It was called the Peace River church of Christ because Punta Gorda was located along the Peace River that flowed into the Gulf of Mexico. I loved that name, Peace River. The whole area was along the shore line of the Gulf of Mexico. Just a little north was Sarasota, and just a little south was Fort Myers.

I flew down, and they offered me the job, but I figured we were $700.00 apart in respect to the move from Texas to Florida. I would have to have $700.00 more, just to make the move. They refused to budge a nickel. I was devastated. I went back to where I was staying (with an older widow lady, 10 years my senior), and told her I could not take the job, and why. She said she would loan me the $700.00, and I could pay it out, and to take the job. She wanted Jo and me to come. I believed it was the providence of God at work. I accepted the work, called and told Jo. We were ecstatic. That little church with only about 50 or so members were going to pay us $600.00 per Sunday, and with our Social Security, that meant over $3,000.00 per month. The reason they could do that was because of the "snowbirds."

"Snow birds" were new to me. I could not recall if I had ever heard of them before, but surely, I had. Lots of wealthy people from the cold northern states come south for the winter, and large numbers come to Florida. I could not imagine many members of the church of Christ having that much money. I was told, however, that church attendance in winter often went up from around 40 or 50, to 80, 90, to even 100, sometimes. The contribution in winter was substantial (I don't remember an amount).

The church had only one Bible class for adults, and one for children. There was one couple that had 2 young teens. Their parents taught their class, and the preacher was to teach all adults in the auditorium Sunday mornings, and Wednesday night.

I met the young man who had been preaching for them, and he was just tired of preaching for them. He was a school teacher in his 20s and had a twin brother. They claimed to be fraternal twins, but sure looked identical.

The young preacher told me that there was another church of Christ about a mile away, but just across the Peace River Bridge in Port Charlotte. He said it was a larger congregation, with about 100 members, and in winter, jumped to more than 200. I asked why the two did not merge? He said that the Punta Gorda people would not cross the bridge to go into Port Charlotte. I could never understand why. Punta Gorda was a small city. Port Charlotte was a "bedroom community" kind of suburb to Punta Gorda, unincorporated, but with 125,000 residents.

When I flew back home, Jim was out of a job and came down from Dallas to help us pack a U-Haul truck, and with the help of some church members, we got our things packed. We traded our little Ford for a larger 4 door Oldsmobile. Jim drove the truck, and I drove our car with Jo along beside me, and off we went to Florida.

I had rented a modest 3-bedroom 2 bath house on a corner lot in Port Charlotte before I came back from Florida, so when we arrived, Jim and I and Jo, and only one church member showed up to help us unload. I had not thought about all the men of the congregation being so much older than I. The member that showed up, was much younger, not a lot older than Jim. It turned out that the vast majority of the church was at least 10 years older than Jo and I. Nearly everybody in Florida was at least 10 years older than Jo and I.

Jim found a job with Blockbusters and worked his way up to assistant manager. He stayed with us trying to save enough money to get back to Texas and find a job there. He later got a really good job managing medical supplies for a group of doctors. Eventually he saved enough to get back to Dallas. I tried everything I could think of to help the little church to grow, but nothing worked.

I forgot to tell about Joe. In 1993, Joe married a girl named Karen and they had a wonderful little boy they named Andrew Wyeth Norman just over a year later in 1994. Karen had a young daughter by a previous marriage.

I got the idea of writing a weekly religious column every Saturday for the local newspaper. I wanted to write about the Bible, but I was not sure I could come up with a column every week. I decided to write a few to see if I could write them weekly, and to see if I had that much to say about the Bible. And then, how long would my column be, and could I keep it the same length week after week.

I started writing, and in a fairly short time, I wrote 52 columns, a year's worth, and all of them were within 300 to 325 words each. I took them to the Newspaper's editor, and presented them to him, telling him what I had done. I did not want pay, and I could not pay the paper. I did not tell him I had 52 columns already written, but I gave him 3 month's-worth. He said he would think about it and get back to me. About two weeks later he called me in, and we had a deal. I called my column, "DICKTATIONS by Dick Norman." It ran the whole 5 years we lived in Florida, but it produced no controversy, no new members, nothing. I could not believe it, but I loved writing it.

I found out that there was a Symphony Orchestra in Fort Myers, just 30 miles south of us, and they had a chorus. I auditioned, and got in. The conductor of the Symphony Orchestra was also the assistant conductor of the Metropolitan Opera Orchestra in New York.

I enjoyed singing with the South Florida Symphony Orchestra Chorus. Among the many things I sang over the 5 years I sang with the chorus was Beethoven's 9th, "Ode To Joy." It would be my 9th time to perform Beethoven's 9th with a Symphony Orchestra. I really love singing it.

Tex's and Kathie's son, Ryan, graduated from high school with honors in 1997, in fact, it was a struggle between Ryan and a girl for the top spot of Valedictorian. It seemed to go back and forth between them, until finally, an nth of a point, they gave it to the girl, and Ryan was Salutatorian. Never mind, however, Ryan got a full scholarship to Princeton University where he worked for and received a Ph.D. in Microbiology. We are so proud to have a grandson so smart and so handsome. The first Norman to get a Phd.

It seemed to rain every afternoon in Florida for about a half hour, a real downpour of around an inch of rain. The soil in Florida was virtually all very sandy, but grass grew profusely. Even just after a rain, ground was not muddy.

One Wednesday night, a young couple came to our services. Leading her parents was the cutest little girl I had seen in a very long time. Her daddy was one of the biggest men I have ever seen. (I can't say she was the cutest, because I had the cutest little daughter, and I can't say her daddy was the tallest, because I have seen several men over 7'.) She was awfully cute, and her daddy was 6'9". They were Bennett and Linda and little Christina Pendergrass. A wonderful Christian family. They became our very best friends.

Our new "best friends" had not lived in Florida long until one day they came over to our house for a visit with us and told us they had to move back to Tennessee. We were very sad to hear that, but we were shocked to hear they wanted us to buy their house. We had visited in their house several times, and were in awe of the incredible beauty and size, etc. It was waaaaaay out of our league. It had about 3,000 sq. ft. floor space, a two car garage, carpeted, and a huge lanai that stretched across the entire back of the house. Sliding glass doors opened in every room across the back of the house so that the whole house opened into the screened-in lanai that covered a beautiful swimming pool and hot-tub. The hot-tub had a small waterfall into the swimming pool. The swimming pool was heated. The house was so wonderfully large and perfectly arranged. The master bedroom was huge, and one wall had glass doors that opened, sliding into the whole wall, and into the lanai and pool. It was like a movie star's home – a rich person's home. We could not possibly buy such a home.

Our friends insisted that we could. They asked how much we paid for rent, and I told them. Then they asked how much we paid for utilities. I told them. Then they told us they had done everything possible to reduce the utilities on their house, and I don't remember what they paid for utilities, but it was a fraction of what we paid. He then said, "You are already paying enough to make the payments on our house." We worked out the deal and moved into the most beautiful and wonderful house. We really enjoyed that pool and that house. That really made the rest of our stay in Florida wonderful.

Jo and I went to the beach at Sarasota several times, and before Jim moved back to Dallas, he went on a cruise. We drove him down to Miami and got lost in Miami on our way home. We found ourselves in a very scary part of Miami and were afraid we would not get out alive. Fortunately, however, we did. We did not want to do that again, and when we went back to pick Jim up, we did alright finding our way home.

I also began writing religious article's and submitting them to the Gospel Advocate. The editor liked my articles very much and printed each one I submitted. The Gospel Advocate is a monthly periodical, and one year, my articles appeared in every issue but one. I guess, because, one month I neglected to send one.

While we were living in Florida, I developed cataracts, and had them removed and replaced with implant lenses – the left eye is for close-up reading, and the right eye is for distance. They work perfectly, and I didn't wear glasses any more until I was 85.

September 22, 1999, we celebrated our 50th wedding anniversary all by ourselves. Our kids were scattered

50TH WEDDING GLAMOUR PHOTO

everywhere, and we knew it was impossible to get our family together for a celebration in Florida.

I found a "Glamor Photographer" in the mall, and our pictures were my present to Jo.

While we still lived in Florida, Jodie, Carol's daughter, graduated from Mount Dora Christian High School in Mount Dora, Florida were her dad preached. Soon after that, she was married there as well.

The whole time we lived in Florida, the weather was great. I wore a suit to services, but never wore a jacket or coat in winters. When we moved we did not own winter clothes.

We never saw a hurricane the whole time we lived in Florida. One came close one time, but no damage was done.

Jo' mother, and mine were growing very old, and we decided we needed to move back to Texas. I began looking for churches looking for preachers in Texas.

I found a church in Seymour, a small country town fairly close to Wichita Falls, and it was right on the highway to Lubbock. So we decided to take a vacation, and drive to Lubbock. I wrote the church I was interested in and sent them a résumé. I told them I would be in their area on their highway on a certain date and asked them if I could stop by for a preaching appointment and interview with them for the job. I did, and they hired me. The year was 2000. We moved there in late summer; I was 70 years old.

We had other photos made, and one is in a little frame with a black and white photo of our wedding.

Our friends moved back to Florida later, but they just bought a different house. When we moved from Florida, our friends bought the house back.

OUR 50TH WEDDING ANNIVERSARY

Chapter 24

We move back to Texas

The church at Seymour paid for our move back to Texas. Seymour, Texas had been an "oil boom town" at one time, but now it had dwindled down to a very small farming community. The church, during the "boom" years, had grown to nearly 400 members, and had built a nice large building to accommodate the crowds. Now, it too, had dwindled down, and now had only about 125.

The little 3-bedroom house the church owned and provided for us free of charge, had been re-painted and repaired as good as they could do, but it quickly developed cracks in the walls, and all kinds of problems. It looked to me like it had been designed by a carpenter. Any visitor who came to the front door would have a clear straight shot view into the main bathroom of the house.

Just after moving to Seymour, I took our old Oldsmobile to a Ford dealer in Wichita Falls (just 30 miles north of Seymour) and traded it for a one-year-old Ford Taurus. It was a great car, one of the best I ever owned. The two best cars I ever owned were Fords, the big 9 passenger Ford Country Squire station wagon, and the Taurus. I loved those cars.

Our granddaughter, Natalie, John's daughter, graduated from Plano East high school the next year, 2001, but we were not able to attend.

Both our mothers died while we lived in Seymour. My mother was living in a nursing home in Waco, Texas, when she died peacefully in her sleep. The year was 2003. She lived to be 94, and she died of old age. My sister, Pat Combs was living in Waco at the time, and was looking after her just as she had looked after our father when he passed. I owe my sister so much in gratitude. My mother had a sharp mind, and a quick wit, and was very active for her age up to her death.

The time came while we lived in Seymour, that we brought Jo's mother from Cameron, Texas, to live with us in Seymour. It was not long until she had to be hospitalized. Three days later, we placed her in a very fine nursing home in Munday, Texas, about 50 miles from Seymour. Jo visited her mother every day until she got so ill she had to go back to the hospital where she died. She was 94.

I was hired in Seymour *because* I was old. I had a lot of experience dealing with troubled churches, I had told them that when I interviewed, and they really liked my "interview" sermons, because I spoke with authority – not mine, but Biblical authority. Of course, everybody loved Jo immediately.

All the elders they had previously had resigned. Why? I don't know, and I told the congregation publicly, in a sermon that if anybody came to me and started to tell me what old brother or sister so-and-so said about so-and-so, I would tell them I don't know, and I don't want to know, and if you tell me, you are a double-tongued, backbiting vulture. I told them we were going to do all we could to "keep the unity of the spirit in the bond of peace" (Eph.4:3).

God told me what to do, and how to do it in Titus 1:5, "set in order the things that are lacking, and appoint elders." I went straight to work, preaching sermons that would set in order the things that were lacking (mostly love and forgiveness), and in 3 months, we appointed elders (that the congregation had selected and approved).

The church of Christ is the body of Christ (I Cor.12:27). The way we treat the church of Christ is the way we treat the body of Christ. The writer of the book of Hebrews said it is even possible to crucify Christ again (Heb.6:6). Spiritually speaking, he said we, today, can crucify Christ by our rejection of Him. I do not want to be guilty of abusing or even bringing reproach on Christ's body, the church of Christ today.

I also told them it was serious business to "badmouth" an elder (I Tim.5:19).

Over the five years we lived there, I had many members come to me and tell me that the church was about to blow up in a thousand pieces before I came, and that I saved it from tearing itself to pieces. I believe it was the providence of God that we went to Seymour to work with that church.

Carol's son, Richard, graduated high school in 2003, in Tavares, but we did not make the trip to see him graduate.

While we were living in Seymour, Tim's and Sue's son Nicholas was graduated from High school in Lubbock. We went to Lubbock to attend his graduation ceremonies. And in 2005, Nicholas was graduated from Lubbock Christian University, which we also got to attend.

While we lived in Dallas, I sang with the Symphony Chorus 10 years. In Florida, I sang 5 years with the South Florida Symphony Chorus. I sang also with choruses in Corpus Christi, New Orleans and Waco, and while we lived in this little Texas town of Seymour, I drove all the way to Wichita Falls, Texas (about 50 miles) to sing with their chorus for 7 years (5 years in Seymour, and 2 in Wichita Falls).

I found a good voice teacher in Wichita Falls. Yes, she was "pretty," in fact, she was beautiful. I took voice lessons from her the 5 years I preached for that church. She was a very good teacher. I was a little surprised she accepted me as a pupil; an old man in his 70s.

I had a bad case of kidney stones there just before we moved to Wichita Falls. I had a bad case when I was 20, in Austin, and another when I was about 40 or so. (Kidney stones was not my voice problem, however.)

I preached for that church 5 years. One Sunday Jo said, "look at this Church." We were standing in the auditorium after the morning worship. People were everywhere talking to each other, and worship services had been over at least 20 minutes. She said, "When we first came here, everybody would be gone in 5 minutes after services, but now, they visit with each other." The church was at peace when we left.

One day I was approached by two board members of a very large nursing home in Wichita Falls. One was the Chairman of the Board. "The Board of Directors were all elders of one congregation. They offered me the job of being the Chaplain for the nursing home, Texoma Christian Care Center. They promised to take "real good care of me." They would give me a place to live on campus free, utilities paid. I would get one free meal a day for Jo and me, and many other "perks" beside a very good salary. Where else could a 75-year-old man get a better deal than that? I took the job. It was the summer of 2005.

Chapter 25

When I grow up...
I want to be a chaplain in a
nursing home...
Really?

The Texoma Christian Care Center has a very large, beautiful campus with very a nice, large building complex. There are two circular buildings housing offices, nursing facilities, storage, and other rooms and offices as needed – all in a big circular configuration. Extending out from the big circular building, are long hallways with rooms for nursing home residents. The two complexes can accommodate about 250 residents. It is one of the nicest and best run nursing homes I have ever seen. Jo and I said that when the time came, we would just move from our campus cottage into the nursing home.

A Non-Profit Corporation
300 Loop 11
Wichita Falls, Texas
940-723-8420

On campus, they had built six of the nicest, and very expensive cottages you would want to have. Ours was really nice and comfortable. We had to "downsize" to get in it.

TCCC, as they often refer to themselves, are affiliated and supported by churches of Christ, but not exclusively. It is run by members of the church, but not exclusively. Lots of our brothers and sisters in Christ work there and are residents there.

I had no job description, because they had never had a chaplain before and did not have a clear idea as to what all my duties would be. They knew they wanted me to conduct a worship service on Sundays and visit with the residents. That was about it. It was up to me to set the standard.

As long as I was preaching in Seymour, I felt young and vigorous, but the very day the movers were packing the truck, I began gathering some things and packing them into a box when all of a sudden, my left arm began to ache, and I felt terrible. I realized it was a symptom of a coming heart attack, so I immediately lay down on my right side, and stayed there for some time, very still. When I got up I felt better, but after our move to Wichita Falls, I never felt as vigorous as I had before. I never mentioned that to anyone until now.

I still had kidney stone problems after our move and spent the first few days in the hospital in Wichita Falls.

My office was directly across the hall from the Director's office. My office was very small. It hardly had enough bookshelves for my books. I had to store some of my books and gave some away.

I set the Sunday worship services in order, enlisting the help of area congregations of churches of Christ (this took several months to get it all working smoothly and orderly). I developed my own sermon style for the residents that would be attending, adjusting the content and the length so that with the singing, prayers and communion service, the entire service was only 40 minutes tops.

My first year, I roamed the halls, trying to meet, and get to know all the residents. If they wanted me to visit with them, I would set a time convenient for them. If they wanted a Bible study, I would have done that, but none ever did. I did make visits to read stories to some of them, and to some, I read the Bible.

As soon as possible after we moved to Wichita Falls, we placed our church membership with the largest congregation in town, Faith Village. They had about 750 members, and plenty of room to grow in their nice new building. I was asked to lead singing often and enjoyed doing it. The congregation was very complimentary of my song leading ability. I was asked to preach on several occasions, and my preaching was also very well received. I was asked to teach the auditorium Bible class, and I was very well received in that as well. I taught my series of studies on "The New Testament Church."

We were so proud of our granddaughter, Natalie, John's daughter, when she was graduated from Texas State University in San Marcos, Texas, with a double major in 2006. She had a Bachelor's in English, and a Bachelor's in Communications. We were so sorry we were not able to go to her graduation ceremonies.

I had been singing in the Community Chorus since we moved to Seymour, and we sang classical music, performing with a Community Symphony Orchestra. For the tenth time I sang in a performance of Beethoven's 9th symphony.

Then, when I was 78, the chorus was to sing Mendelssohn's Elijah, and our director asked for open auditions to sing the bass solos as Elijah. I auditioned along with about seven other basses. Our director asked me and a young voice major at Midwestern University in Wichita Falls to audition again. Our director listened to the two of us again and again, until he finally chose the student over me. I was devastated. I believed I was the better choice, and I had never soloed before. I believed this was my last opportunity in my life. I was so upset that I quit singing in the chorus (after I sang the piece with the chorus).

Toward the middle of our second year in Wichita Falls, things began to take a downward turn. I began having a difficult time walking. I would make a tour of a couple of halls, and I would have to go back to my office and rest a bit before going on a trip through another hall or two. Each building had five long halls, but at this point, TCCC was only using one building, and was renting out the other building. I began to have trouble with my voice when I went to my voice lessons. There was something in my throat that came up into my vocal chords whenever I tried to sing, and I could not get it out. I went to doctors, and they tried all kinds of medications, but nothing worked. It got so bad, I could not lead singing at church any more, and I got to where I could not sing at all. My walking problem got so bad that they got me a scooter to make my rounds on.

One Sunday morning I was asked to preach, and it seemed I was unable to think quickly on my feet. My sermons are all written out, so I had no real problem completing the sermon. However, I usually am able to deliver them as though I am just speaking them and not reading them. But then, when I started down the steps from the pulpit to the floor, my legs almost gave way. There were about 6 steps, and when I finally got to the floor, it was all I could do to stand in front of the congregation until the invitation song ended and I could sit down.

In the summer of 2006, Jo began having pain in her lower abdomen. The doctor gave her medication, but it did not help. This went on for weeks, until one Saturday afternoon, she began to have such severe pain that I took her to the ER. The young intern took X-rays but saw nothing. He started to just give her some pain pills and send her home, but on a whim, he decided to do a C-scan. What he found put him into action. He called a Cancer Surgeon and set up a surgical room for Jo. He said he saw a 6 to 10-pound tumor in her lower abdomen. They operated on her as soon as possible, it was emergency surgery.

When they were done, the surgeon said he took a 10 pound cancer out of Jo's abdomen, and said he thought he got every bit of it. She had Ovarian Cancer, and the doctor was sending the tumor to Houston's Cancer Center. He said the cancer could come back, but he did not think it would, because he thought he took all of it out.

They gave her a series of chemo treatments to make sure the cancer did not come back. The chemo made her awfully sick in her stomach. She had a terrible time.

I, the eternal optimist, was certain my Jodie was cancer free, but just a few weeks later, we went to M. D. Anderson in Houston, and they told us that there was no hope, that Ovarian Cancer always came back, that it has never been successfully treated, and we should just go home and prepare for her to die.

Sure enough, they took another C-scan, and found a new tumor the size of a ping pong ball. They called in a big name specialist to take it out. He, too, claimed to have gotten it all, and declared her cancer free.

Again, they gave her a series of chemo treatments to try to make sure no cancer would come back. These also made her very sick.

For some time, she seemed to be cancer free, but then, she had another C-scan, and they found a small lump the size of a marble, but they thought it might not be cancer. They refused to take it out but wanted to give her more chemo. Jo said no.

With Jo's problem and my problems with walking and with my voice, we decided it was time we retired. Retirement scared the life out of me. The job I had at TCCC was paying me more than I made preaching at Seymour, what with all the "perks" and all. How could we live on just our Social Security? The reduction in income would be thousands of dollars. We were already getting our Social Security, so we knew exactly how little we would be living on. I don't remember the exact amount now, but it was about $1,600.00.

So, we decided to move to Lubbock, where Tim and Carol lived, so they could look after us in our old age. After all, I was 77, and Jo was 74. We located a small apartment in a retirement community that was just opening up in Lubbock, Hillcrest Manor. And once again we jumped off into thin air, not knowing if we could survive.

John said he would help us financially to be sure we could make it in retirement, which he did, paying hundreds a month for our Medicare supplement until we figured out how to get along without it. He helped us a very long time, I don't recall how long, but we could not have made it without his help.

I retired from TCCC, and they gave me the nicest farewell party anyone could ever want. I felt so blessed to have been the first chaplain at TCCC. I know it was God's providence that Jo and I were there.

For about a year after we moved to Lubbock, I received phone calls and mail from residents from the nursing home that felt they had to keep up with me and tell me how much they loved me. I also received several phone calls from the members of the church in Seymour telling me how much they appreciated my help in saving the congregation from splitting.

Chapter 26

When I grow up...
I want to retire!!

We move to Lubbock...

It was November of 2007. We really had to downsize again to get into the extremely small two-bedroom apartment we rented at Hillcrest Manor. We both still drove, so we rented a garage in which we stored all the things we could not get into the apartment. When we got done, both the garage and the apartment were full.

Our little apartment was wall to wall with boxes floor to ceiling. I could not believe Jo could unpack all of them and find places to put everything, but, in time, she did. All by herself, she did it all, even with the cancer she had. But at this point we really thought she might be cancer free. Like always in our life together, she made the place we lived in comfortable and attractive, and to look like home. She was something very special.

When we were settled into our little apartment, Jo began sewing, and quilting, and making things as fast as she could. She was so talented. She could do and make anything in the world she wanted to do. It was as though she was trying to get things done before she died, and I am sure that was exactly what was on her mind. She was very productive.

Jo tried to make special quilts for each one of her kids and did. She made cloth dolls and sewed pictures to hang on the walls (I don't know what you call them). She was constantly busy, her hands just flying.

We put our church membership in with the brethren at the Parkway Drive church of Christ because Carol's husband, Ron, was the preacher there, and Tim and Sue and Nicholas were members there as well.

When we got settled in to our apartment, we decided we needed to find Jo an Oncologist, and check to see if her little marble size tumor was growing. We found one, and he said her tumor was not growing, and that her cancer appeared to be in remission. However, he wanted her to take a series of chemo treatments. She started them, but they made her so sick, she quit. All her hair fell out and she became as bald as billiard ball, but she never wore a wig, just a small hat, mostly for others, not herself, for she was without vanity and didn't care if she was bald. I still believed her to be the most beautiful woman in the world. She said we would just enjoy the time we had left together and play like she was cancer free. So we did.

I was not doing very well. Jo said she thought I walked like I had Parkinson's. I went to a Neurologist and, sure enough, he said I had A-typical Parkinson's – "non-shaking" Parkinson's. It took away my voice, and my ability to walk very well.

Jodie, our oldest granddaughter, Carol and Ron's oldest child, had a baby boy in 2009. He is our first great-grandchild. Jo was so very thrilled to get to see Tristan and know her first great-grandson. Jodie and Jo were very close as Jodie was named after her grandmother. You see, I called Jo, "Jodie," all her life. It was my "pet name" for my beloved wife, and Carol named her daughter, Jodie.

However, Jo's cancer came back, and she got very sick.

On September 22, 2009, we celebrated our 60th Wedding Anniversary. Friends and family came from everywhere. Jo was very ill and, in the hospital, but her doctor allowed her a day out to attend her Anniversary party. She could barely make it, but she was determined to do so, and did. All of our six children came. Jo was so thrilled to have all her children together around her one last time, and most of their families. It was a wonderful occasion, and we have it on DVD.

She made it past our 61st Anniversary. Jo lived just three short years after we moved to Lubbock. After her cancer came back, all the doctors could do was to try to control her pain and keep her as comfortable as possible. Eventually, she was put under Hospice Care, and she did not last long. Jo died December 22, 2010.

We had some of the most wonderful and happy years together in the later years of our life. Especially from the time we moved to Florida until the day she died.

Florida:

Florida was so wonderful. It was warm all year around. Jo loved the sun. She never would lie out in the sun. She could get tan from a warm breeze. She loved for us to go to the beach in Sarasota, and she made the most of our beautiful pool and hot tub in our backyard. I had fresh grapefruit for breakfast every morning from our trees in our backyard, and also fresh orange juice.

We took long walks together, and talked and laughed, and enjoyed each other. We never saw any bad weather in all the 5 years we lived in Florida. It was a wonderful experience, and we both believed it was the providence of God that led us there.

Seymour, Texas:

We also felt that Seymour was providential for us. Not only in our being able to help a congregation that needed help, but in the wonderful friendships we made there. They gave us "old folks" a sense of purpose and a sense of value. We had lots of good times and good memories in Seymour as well. Just the two of us, our children grown and gone from home, we learned to enjoy just being together.

Wichita Falls:

Our little cottage on the campus of Texhoma Christian Care Center was truly a beautiful little home for just the two of us. Actually, it had much more space than you would imagine just from looking at it from the outside. It was very comfortable to live in.

One of the "perks" of living there was that they brought us lunch every day from the kitchen of the nursing home. It was always delicious. We had only to fix us some breakfast and supper each day, and we did not need much after the big lunch we had.

Another "perk" was that "housekeeping" came once a week to clean our place, so Jo did not have much to do each day, so she quilted, and sewed and made soft dolls and kept busy as though time was running out.

We liked Wichita Falls, and enjoyed our time there as well.

In Wichita Falls, I sang with their community chorus, and found a very good voice teacher. She charged $100,00 an hour for lessons. My last year to live in Wichita Falls, I auditioned to sing the lead role in Mendelssohn's oratorio Elijah, and almost won the competition. At 78, my voice was still that good. A short time after, I began to have coughing fits every time I tried to sing. I stopped voice lessons, and for 10 years I could not sing a note.

Lubbock:

It was wonderful moving to Lubbock to be close to a couple of our kids, Tim and his family, Sue and Nicholas, and Carol and her family, her husband Ron, and son Jordan (Jodie and Richard lived elsewhere). Tim and Carol were going to take care of Jo and me.

Other than Jo's cancer and my Parkinson's, we thoroughly enjoyed our final time together in Lubbock – maybe the best years of our life together. I loved her so deeply, but her love for me was much deeper; she made me feel like I was the luckiest man alive. I believe I was.

Tex and Kathie moved from Florida to Oklahoma City, to be closer to Kathie's mother, and to us. They had a terrible auto accident and lots of problems as a result, but they are settled in now, I guess. Tex has come for a visit, since Jo died, and that was a real treat for me.

Jo and did not go many places, or see much, but we sat side by side in our recliner loveseat, watched a lot of TV, and talked a lot. I found out that even after all these sixty-one years, I could still make her laugh. I kept her laughing and happy as long as I could.

After Jo died, I moved to a small, but extremely comfortable apartment in a retirement complex. My son Tim became an elder of the church Jo and I had been attending. I was in my early 80s, but the church used me to teach Bible classes and preach occasionally.

It was in Lubbock in 2012 that Tex suggested I do some writing. It would give me something to do that would be productive and I wouldn't just sit around and read and watch TV. I was 82. I had done much writing in my life; articles for the Firm Foundation and the Gospel Advocate, my newspaper column in Florida, and my novel in the 980s which never sold. Tex self-published my novel at this point, and it is available for purchase in his online bookstore and in mine now.

First, Tex suggested I write an autobiography, so I did. Tex filled my finished manuscript with illustrations and pictures and self-published it through lulu.com. It is available through Tex's online bookstore and mine.

Then, Tex suggested I write a book about what I believe and why, so I did. I titled the book, AN UNCOMMON MAN. It, too, is available through our online bookstores.

Next, Tex suggested I write a set of commentaries on the entire Bible. After all, the Bible had been a major part of my entire life. I had read it through since I was 12 years old, and in 1964, I began reading it three times a year by reading 10 pages a day. I'd read the Bible well over 150 times at least, plus, I'd taught and preached it since I was 19 years old. I began that project in 2013 at the age of 83, never believing I could live long enough to complete the job. But in 2017, I finished my set of commentaries o the Bible. They were not true commentaries, but mostly just things I'd learned about each book by reading and studying it so many times. My commentaries are more "study guides" that might be useful for Bible teachers. At the age of 88, I have begun rewriting them. I will call the second edition, A Study Guide. I hope to publish my Second Edition on Kindle.

Since I finished my first set of commentaries in December 2017, I have written a book and self-published, A BIBLE SCHOOL DIRECTOR'S MANUAL. I had about 5 years' experience as a Bible school director and taught that subject at several Bible Teacher Training Workshops in many states over a number of years; Jo also teaching teachers of Ladies' Bible Classes. This book is also available in my online bookstore.

I also wrote a book called THE CHURCH JESUS BUILT. It contains 13 chapters and is intended to be a study guide for a Bible class about the church you read about in the New Testament. It could be developed into 13 sermons on that vital subject. It's available in my online bookstore.

Then wrote and self-published a book: MEMOIRS OF A GOSPEL PREACHER which tells of my experiences from the day I decided to begin preaching until 2018. It's in my bookstore also.

All my books in my bookstore sell at cost. My site is lulu.com/spotlight/richardnorman. I have self-published 36 books since 2013.

I am currently making all my books into Second Editions by rewriting, correcting, and updating each book. I hope to publish them all on Kindle.

In the middle of December in 2014, I took very sick. I began having strange sorts of seizures that, I assume now, were hallucinations of dying. I would get to a point I believed I was taking my last breath when suddenly the seizure stopped, and I was fine.

These were so bad I was hospitalized for about a month, and very nearly died several times. After I was released, I went to rehab for about a month. But soon after going back to my apartment, the seizures returned with a vengeance.

In February of 2015, I had 35 seizures, and doctors and my family were convinced that one of those seizures would kill me soon. So, I moved in with my daughter Carol the end of February and lived with her and Ron for about a month and a half. Some of those seizures occurred when I lived with Carol. Every day we all thought I would die in a seizure, so I was put under Hospice Care.

I stayed with Carol and Ron until June 13, 2015 when I moved in with Joe, my youngest son (one of our twins), and we are in our fourth year together.

Moving to the Dallas area, I had to find a new doctor and change my insurance. I chose Dr. Theresa Eichenwald. She did not believe I had Parkinson's disease and sent me to a neurologist who said I'd never had it, and it was all the medication I was taking that made me so sick and was killing me. I was taking 19 prescriptions, and Dr. Eichenwald began weaning me off my prescriptions slowly. As I stopped taking pills, I began to improve dramatically. I was taken off Hospice Care.

When I moved in with Joe, I was still very ill and weak. Now, I'm in perfect health except for vertigo which is so bad I must use a walker. Other than vertigo, there is nothing at all wrong with me. I'm down from 19 pills to 4 and I'm being weaned off another pill that is thought to be the most potent with the side effect of dizziness. We hope I will be able to walk without a walker then. I expect to eventually get off every pill.

After moving in with Joe June 13, 2015, I still could not sing a note without causing a coughing fit. But in May of 2017, I found that I could sing a little in church. My singing voice was returning. Joe wanted me to try singing on his website Sing snap (a karaoke site), so I sang two or three songs. Joe purchased a karaoke Sing snap site for me RNorman1929, and I began making recordings and posting them on my Facebook page. I have to this date recorded almost 400 songs on SINGSNAP, and Joe has uploaded 8 recordings to YouTube, planning to upload more as he can. My recordings have been viewed over 10,000 times. I record something almost every morning.

My voice is not as good as it once was, but not bad for an 88-year-old, and I enjoy making recordings. I have enjoyed singing again. Singing has always been a major part of my life. I had private voice lessons more than 20 years of my life. I once had a vocal range of nearly three octaves, but now less than two. I do not have the great power, versatility, and voice control I had just 10 years ago, but I'm pleased I can now sing again just a little bit. I truly love to sing.

The church we attended three years in Flower Mound let me teach and preach some even at the age of 88. I now attend the West Main church of Christ in Lewisville, and I may have the opportunity to teach and preach a bit. Teaching and preaching God's word has been the joy of my life.

I have lived a wonderful and very happy life, and often feel God blessed me more than anyone. I praise my God daily.

Printed in Great Britain
by Amazon

73404677R00130